Resistance:
An Indigenous Response to Neoliberalism

Resistance:
An Indigenous Response to Neoliberalism

Edited by Maria Bargh

HUIA

First published in 2007 by Huia Publishers
39 Pipitea Street, P O Box 17–335
Wellington, Aotearoa New Zealand
www.huia.co.nz

ISBN 978-1-869692-86-5

Cover design: The Letterheads

National Library of New Zealand Cataloguing-in-Publication Data
Bargh, Maria
Resistance: an indigenous response to neoliberalism / edited by Maria Bargh.
Includes bibliographical references and index.
ISBN 978-1-869692-86-5
1. Neoliberalism. 2. Maori (New Zealand people)—Economic conditions. 3. Maori (New Zealand people)—Politics and government. [1. Tōrangapū.] I. Bargh, Maria, 1977 -
330.122—dc 22

Papa–tu–a–nuku
(Earth Mother)

Hone Tuwhare

We are stroking, caressing the spine
of the land.

We are massaging the ricked
back of the land

with our sore but ever-loving feet:
hell, she loves it!

Squirming, the land wriggles
In delight

We love her.

H. Tuwhare, *Deep River Talk: Collected Poems*, Auckland: Godwit Press Ltd, 1993, p. 126.

Contents

Part Three

Part Four

Acknowledgements

Like many Māori in this country, I am continually astonished by practices and assumptions that dismiss, devalue and dismantle Māori rights. This collection focuses on a particularly dominant strand of these attacks: neoliberal practices and assumptions. I am indebted to the diverse range of activists who have inspired this collection, and whose dedication and sacrifices make it difficult not to keep struggling.

I would like to thank the contributors who have given their time, energy and passion for the chapters in this book, and who have given even more in their work to resist neoliberal practices.

I would like to acknowledge the Macmillan Brown Centre for Pacific Studies at the University of Canterbury, where I was a Research Fellow in late 2004, and where some of the original work for my chapters in this collection was done.

To Huia Publishers, for editorial and other support and for leading the way in independent publishing that encourages Māori and Pacific writers, he mihi nunui. A big thank you also to Anne Else for editorial support and many thanks to all of you who have helped to make this a better book by providing feedback on early drafts and structures.

A special thank you goes to Barry Hindess at the Australian National University, who was the supervisor for my PhD, from which I have drawn much material for this book. Thank you, Barry, for all your inspiration.

A big mihi to Aotearoa Educators (AE!) for maintaining a steady, stimulating and vibrant activist unit, often across substantial geographical areas, including Korea, China, Australia, the Czech Republic, South Africa and Bolivia.

Huge aroha to my friends and whānau, with whose support this has been made possible. You have all helped navigate me through and put up with so much on the way: tirades on oppression and hypocrisies, decolonisation and resistance, continuous draft papers/chapters/speeches/lectures, schemes for dressing-up in public as everything from a sandcastle to a star, paint cans, laughter and tears. Arohapounamu ki a koutou.

Ki ōku tūpuna, arā, koutou kua wheturangitia, nā koutou anō tōku ara i whakamārama. Tēnā rawa atu koutou, āwhina tonu mai. Ko te tumanako, ka rite tēnei mahi ōku ki tētahi puna wai, mā reira e whai kaha ai ngā toa o ngā rā kei te heke mai. To my ancestors who have become the stars, you have also helped me on this path. Thank you. I look forward to your continued support. The hope is that this work will be like a spring that will help strengthen others in days yet to come.

And finally to everyone everywhere resisting neoliberalism and continued colonisation, kia kaha; we will need it.

Maria Bargh
Wellington, 2007

Introduction

Resistance: an indigenous response to neoliberalism
The advance of neoliberalism, despite overwhelming evidence of its failures, has encouraged the compilation of this collection. There is an urgent need to document not only examples of overt Māori resistance to neoliberal policies, but also more subtle stories of activities which implicitly challenge neoliberal practices and assumptions by their support for other ways of living.

Before exploring examples of resistance and challenges to neoliberalism, neoliberal practices and policies must first be defined. There is already a vast amount of work on neoliberal practices. For the purposes of this book, neoliberalism will be defined as those practices and policies which seek to extend the market mechanism into areas of the community previously organised and governed in other ways. This process involves the entrenching of the three central tenets of neoliberalism: 'free' trade and the 'free' mobility of capital, accompanied by a broad reduction in the ambit and role of the state.

Several of the authors in this collection use a number of terms interchangeably for neoliberalism, such as globalisation, neoliberal globalisation, or the New Right. Others talk about neoliberal practices as a new form of colonisation. They are all discussing policies and practices which are very similar, if not exactly the same. While globalisation involves a range of activities beyond neoliberal practices, neoliberal practices and assumptions are often seen as dominant in globalisation. For example, the increased flow of goods and services which many people highlight as a feature of globalisation is entangled with neoliberal aims for 'free' trade and 'free' mobility of capital. Many indigenous peoples view the way that neoliberal practices maintain this dominance as akin to colonisation.

In this introductory chapter, I begin by examining the central features of neoliberalism and its justifications. The justifications most commonly advanced are that the market is the most efficient way to organise human interactions, and that economic growth equals human improvement. These rest on particular assumptions about people, including indigenous peoples. Secondly, I explore how these assumptions, made by neoliberal advocates about indigenous peoples, reflect long-standing Western ideas that were manifested in colonisation, and which highlight connections between colonial and neoliberal practices. A number of the authors in this collection refer to neoliberalism as a new form of colonisation. Given these understandings of neoliberalism, in the final section of this chapter I look at how resistance becomes shaped in part by what is being resisted: through decolonisation. Resistance and challenges to neoliberal practices also come simply from Māori living and maintaining alternative world-views. Neoliberal practices seek to extend the market mechanism everywhere; communities or parts of communities which ignore or subvert neoliberal practices therefore create and sustain lives that neoliberals cannot control.

'Free' trade

The first of the three central tenets of neoliberalism is 'free' trade, which relies on the theory of comparative advantage. Most Western economists, not simply neoliberal advocates, now argue that all countries can benefit from trade through comparative advantage; that is, they need to specialise in the production and export of those goods which they can produce at relatively low cost, and import those goods which are expensive for them to produce, provided that the goods are able to move freely across borders. This perception is of 'free' trade as a discrete practice, not as an inherent part of policies designed to advance political or more broadly imperial purposes.[1] Neoliberal advocates claim that it is more efficient for countries to specialise and trade than to produce all goods themselves with closed borders.

When the neoliberal ideas about trade and comparative advantage were first formulated in the early 1800s, it was still relatively difficult to engage in capital transactions across borders.[2] At that time, capital did not flow freely from one country to another.[3] The expansion of financial markets in the early 1900s, and the current explosion of financial markets which now transact billions of dollars daily, make this part of neoliberal comparative advantage theory redundant.[4] In addition, the ideas of the 1800s relied on assumptions that countries had full employment and a balance of trade in each trading country, and that it was not possible to move either capital or production facilities easily across borders.[5] These conditions, too, are no longer applicable; transnational corporations (TNCs) can quite quickly move their factories from one country to another, with no particular loyalties to individual states. From this perspective, comparative advantage theory rests upon a paradox: it depends on fixed national borders, but these do not fit with the permeable borders required for the neoliberal conception of 'free' trade. Given the current shape of world affairs, the continued relevance of comparative advantage theory is questionable; yet neoliberal advocates continue to insist on its pre-eminence.

'Free' mobility of capital

According to neoliberal advocates, 'free' mobility of capital is also an essential requirement for development and growth. For 'developed' countries, investment maintains existing conditions and promotes more growth. For 'developing' countries, which neoliberals see as severely deficient in capital, investment is argued to be the key requirement for the initial 'take-off' towards development and growth. For developing countries, investment comes from several sources: from governments as official development aid; from foreign direct investment; and from institutions as loans.[6]

While some neoliberals can tolerate government-to-government official development assistance, to the majority of neoliberals, this is often perceived as too much like 'free' money, amounting to a welfare 'handout' to countries which have not 'worked' for it. For neoliberals, such financial 'hand-outs' can be dangerous, because not forcing people to work in order to benefit encourages dependency.

Some neoliberals have been encouraging the reduction of official development aid, arguing instead for the benefits achievable from foreign direct investment from TNCs.[7] The activities of TNCs as the principal providers of direct investment are often welcomed by these neoliberals, who assume this movement to be a strong component of the efficiency of the private sector, using investment in the market far more efficiently than a government ever could. The impetus towards and increases in foreign direct investment flows often parallel the privatisation of government-owned assets. However, the movement of investment between developed and developing countries has not occurred in the way that neoliberal theorists have predicted. Neoliberals argue that for developing countries, '(f)oreign direct investment can bring not only much needed additional capital but also access to technology and know-how, as well as access to international markets';[8] but often it appears that this is not the case.

The United Nations 1999 Human Development Report estimated that more than \$1.5 trillion is now exchanged on the world currency markets each day, and that foreign direct investment flows have also increased. However these transactions have remained predominately within Organisation for Economic Cooperation and Development (OECD) countries.[9] Many scholars in the Pacific argue that technology transfers occur more often through aid than through private enterprises, and those that do come from TNCs, for example, are often "mature" and not up to the latest standards.[10] Furthermore, as Martin Khor argues, the types of technologies which are transferred to developing countries more often constitute hazardous technologies exploiting lax or nonexistent safety and environmental regulations.[11] Foreign investment, therefore, does not always produce the kind of economic benefits claimed by neoliberals.

Among the various institutions which provide 'investment', particularly for developing countries, the World Bank and International Monetary Fund (IMF) are perhaps the most significant. While the World Bank provides loans specifically for development purposes, the IMF's mandate has more to do with maintaining the stability of capital flows than with promoting development as such. The IMF's specific aim of maintaining 'stability' leads to expanding and encouraging foreign direct investment and providing capital input, i.e. loans, which are intended to promote and ensure:

international monetary cooperation...facilitate the expansion and balanced growth of international trade...promote exchange stability...assist in the establishment of a multilateral system of payments...and...shorten the duration and lessen the degree of disequilibrium in the international balance of payments of members.[12]

In short, the IMF is not a development organisation, but an institution whose key purpose is to ensure stability so that the international financial system continues, balances of payments are protected and world trade can grow.

A significant issue which the IMF has continually failed to address is the opposition to their now infamous Structural Adjustment Policies (SAPs). These policies impose conditionalities on states, such as privatisation of state assets, in exchange for investment funds. SAPs are an overt mechanism to embed neoliberal policies. Despite widespread condemnation of these kinds of policies as a 'one size fits all' model, as inappropriate when applied locally en masse, and as encouraging large-scale projects which are often environmentally and socially destructive, the IMF responds that these are actually chosen by countries.[13] The inability of the IMF to change these SAPs or comprehend the importance of the criticism directed against them demonstrates rigidity in approaching issues and peoples, as well as inability to understand the inconsistencies in IMF tenets and policies.

The contradiction in the neoliberal quest for 'freer' capital mobility is that, in a very real way, this increases the risks involved for those who feel the effects when corporate investors use the tools of finance to gamble in a 'casino economy'.[14] The mobility of capital has encouraged the development of financial instruments and communications technologies that enable this market to operate and flourish. It is this market which, some theorists argue, has shifted investment away from productive activities into mere speculation, which in turn detaches financial markets from social concerns and social consequences. Some have suggested that:

> The ascendancy of electronic money has shifted the function of finance from investing to transacting, enhancing the attractiveness of speculation (e.g. in national currencies) rather than direct investments in productive capacity, and institutionalising the volatility in the process.[15]

David Korten argues that this leads 'financial markets and the owners of capital [to] become...detached from social concerns and abstracted from practical realities of commerce'.[16] When the financial markets are detached in this way from the ramifications of speculative practices, these ramifications become merely 'adjustment costs'.[17] This is where neoliberals point to the IMF and suggest it needs to tinker a little with government regulations in order to support countries which might be susceptible to casino economics, thus ensuring their stability in a particular way. The central point here is that neoliberals fail to see the enormity of the contradiction.

Reducing the size of the state
The third major tenet of neoliberal practices is reducing the size of the state. Neoliberal policies seek to strictly limit the ambit of the state in particular ways. These include the corporatisation and privatisation of many government assets, and the corporatisation of both the remaining state assets and the culture of the public service.[18] For neoliberals, the state should be involved in regulating the provision of goods and services only if absolutely necessary,

and if so, in a form which is amenable to market interaction and transactions.

The policies of privatisation and corporatisation have perhaps been the most visible signs of neoliberalism in New Zealand since 1984. Privatisation is one of the simplest avenues by which to achieve a large reduction of the ambit of the state. Privatisation fulfils three functions at once: 'It expands the market; it shifts emphasis from public to private purposes; and it reduces the size of government by stripping it of the resources that allow regulation and intervention'.[19]

The rationale behind privatisation is that, 'Private enterprise should be allowed to function competitively and not be crowded-out by the public sector.'[20] One problem with this assumption is that in the 'free' market, it is not likely to be locally-owned companies that win contracts or are able to afford to buy government assets. These contracts and enterprises are more likely to be bought by TNCs who have the recources to be 'competitive'.

While neoliberal advocates see much state regulation as negative, they argue that the state does have a vital role in providing defence, law and order, and particularly a sound legal system to protect contract and property rights. Additionally, they argue that inter-state institutions, and the agreements they formulate within these institutions, play an important role in further reducing the role of the state and embedding policies of 'free' trade and 'free' capital mobility. Neoliberal advocates see institutions such as the World Trade Organisation (WTO), IMF and World Bank as able to provide a mechanism by which those countries particularly in 'need' of neoliberal policies can have them introduced and monitored, even as they simultaneously reduce the size of the state.

In this way, the international agreements founded on neoliberal policies are used to increasingly limit the ability that the state has to modify or reverse these same policies. Some scholars argue that this is a positive development, as it 'will make it very difficult for successor governments to reverse them'.[21] The World Bank argues that these agreements 'lock-in benefits'.[22] The policies which these agreements enshrine are designed to withstand, for example, changes of government that might disrupt the 'continuity' of the policies, or potentially do away with them altogether.

There are two central justifications which underscore the three core tenets of neoliberal policies: that the market is efficient, and that economic growth equals human improvement.

Justification one: the market is efficient

Neoliberal advocates view the market as a positive and productive mechanism to regulate the interaction of individuals, to civilise, and to encourage peace. Neoliberal policies are justified on the basis that the market is generally more efficient at 'enhancing individual freedom', or, to put it another way, better at governing the interaction of individuals, than any other system of 'regulation', especially that imposed by the state.

According to neoliberals, the market's potential for creating social harmony stems from its natural and orderly nature. Advocates argue that the market is spontaneous in its operation; it is self-creating and could be self-regulating if not interfered with. As Frederich Hayek argues, 'to understand our civilisation, one must appreciate that the extended order resulted not from human design or intention but spontaneously...'[23] The market is not anarchic, but ordered by certain laws, or as Adam Smith puts it, by 'the invisible hand'.[24] The laws of the market are perceived by neoliberals to be objectively observable laws of nature that exist in the world. Trading is seen to occur in the market place, where the market is seen as a machine that, once established, 'glides along, each component part contributing to its serene process'.[25] The market supposedly encourages more production in response to greater demand, and limits supply in response to lesser demand.[26]

Like the individual pursuit of self-interest, the market is seen, above all, as being impersonal and as enhancing the freedom of the individual. In the market, it is claimed, '(w)ith the exception of rare and necessarily transitory monopolies, no one exercises control. Each participant is equally subject to the same impersonal forces.

Outcomes are not the result of any *one* person's or group's actions or will.'[27] In this way, all individuals are equal in the eyes of the market. What is assumed by neoliberals is that people are acting voluntarily in the marketplace, and that while they may at times be forced to make 'difficult' decisions, these are made of their own free choice. Neoliberal advocates claim that difficult options, or a limited number of options, is not the crucial issue, as 'freedom has nothing to say about what an individual does with his [sic] freedom…a major aim of the liberal is to leave the ethical problem for the individual to wrestle with'.[28] The individual's 'freedom of choice does not include the idea that there will, or should be, a tolerable alternative, though there is always the existential choice between life and death'.[29] Neoliberals essentially take the status quo of social and political economic relations in society as impermeable, and leave individuals to their fate. This assumption arises because neoliberals equate 'free' with 'voluntary':

> In another example of either/or thinking, voluntary behaviour is the opposite of being coerced. All behaviour that is not coerced is free, voluntary, and self-chosen.…It assumes that each person in an 'economic' relation is an autonomous, self-directing actor and views freedom from the perspective of the person acting, not the person acted upon. The notion of being acted upon – by manipulation, compulsion, subliminal suggestion, or passive receipt of externalities – hardly exists in this thinking. People outside market transactions are not considered.[30]

While neoliberal advocates call for individuals to be left to their own choices, so that the market can respond to these choices, they fail to pay much attention to how 'needs' and 'wants' actually function in the marketplace. Neoliberals suggest that the market responds to 'supply and demand', but the market does not necessarily respond to people's demands in the form of needs. Instead the market responds to money and those who have the power and privileges to pay for their wants. If people are denied access to their basic needs, the market does not assist them or intervene to create a better livelihood for them. Neoliberals respond to such criticisms by reasserting that those individuals who do participate in the market are helping the needs and wants of others by generally creating wealth which will eventually be redistributed. That is, they suggest that individual self-interest will contribute to the greater good by creating wealth that will 'trickle down'.[31]

Neoliberal policies and practices largely ignore a whole array of claims about discrimination in the functioning of the marketplace, such as racism. If such 'prejudices' do exist, neoliberals argue, they will be overcome by market forces. If they are not, then they must in some sense be 'natural'. Neoliberals see the state as the most likely and significant source of trampling on political and economic freedoms. Advocates argue that:

> Fundamentally, there are only two ways of co-ordinating the economic activities of millions. One is central direction involving the use of coercion – the technique of the army and the modern totalitarian state. The other is voluntary co-operation of individuals – the technique of the market place.[32]

The negative perception here of the state is that it is most likely to have a tendency for monopoly and 'artificial' control, as opposed to the natural functioning of the market. The state is perceived as impinging on a market which works most efficiently with minimal interference, but where the state is needed to act as a preliminary instigator of the 'rules of the game'.[33] After the correct kind of environment has been set up, however, neoliberals remain convinced that the state always distorts economic performance thereafter, because it interferes with the 'natural' market mechanism.

Justification two: economic growth equals human improvement

The long-term goal and justification of neoliberal policies is 'economic growth', that is, an increase in the aggregate national income. It is claimed that this will increase the wellbeing of all people. For neoliberals, economic growth equates to development, and eventually to better standards of living.

Growth for neoliberal advocates means essentially 'economic growth', or even more specifically, 'real movements in the amount of goods and services which are produced, or real movements in material living standards'.[34] To gauge whether or not a country is achieving 'growth', or showing any signs of emerging from poverty and developing, neoliberals use increases in Gross Domestic Product (GDP) as their measure. As a measuring tool, GDP contains numerous flaws, such as being unable to perceive the distribution of wealth within countries, the long-term consequences of transactions, differences between 'good' and 'bad' transactions, and transactions occurring 'outside' the market.[35] It is important to note that all indicators used in attempts to measure improvements, whether they concern economic growth, reductions in poverty or a multitude of other political, economic or social conditions, are infinitely problematic. If such indicators are to be used, however, then the ways in which they are each inadequate and the purposes for which they are being used must be considered.

The key institutions using GDP as a measure of human improvement, the World Bank, IMF and WTO, dismiss claims that they are 'killing the planet' and perpetuating the 'globalisation of poverty',[36] instead arguing that the quest for economic development is fundamentally about fighting for 'a world free of poverty'.[37] Constructing the argument in this manner means that the categorisation of the 'problem' essentially lies with 'poverty', and this shifts the focus away from the wealthy, who benefit from the exploitation of the planet and of other people to maintain their privileged positions.[38] Given the neoliberal faith in the equilibrating and fair nature of the market, the cause of poverty becomes a lack of access to the market, the solution to which can then simplistically be the provision of market access to poor individuals.

As the culmination of neoliberalism's prescriptions and foundations, the pursuit of economic growth as 'development' suggests that broader and deeper questions should be asked about processes of cultural homogenisation, and about the interaction between local and international forces. Development in this sense is more about governing the 'exporting and importing of culture' than merely 'raising standards of living'. Most neoliberals do not deny such a connection; they merely claim that it is all 'worth it', and point to research which, when narrowly interpreted, supports their assertions, such as the fact that world growth has increased over recent decades.[39]

At the heart of neoliberalism are assumptions about the individual and the market as having particular natural identities. Being conceived as 'objectively' discovered and known as the best option for the future in this way gives neoliberalism on one level a way of dismissing alternatives without great consideration of them.

The 'factual' scientific claim implicitly made for neoliberal arguments is indeed persuasive, appealing to an entrenched discourse which emphasises a set of theories and practices conceptualised in nineteenth century Britain. For those state makers in need of solutions to 'problems' which are often framed as such by neoliberals, the political, economic and intellectual pressure from other governments, economists and the business sector to succumb to neoliberal prescriptions is great. In the course of their prescriptions for the economic development of countries, neoliberals and neoliberal institutions have taken on something of a dictatorial role. According to neoliberals, their ideas are positive for humanity. This means that they fervently believe that their prescriptions are not only right, but that they have the 'right' or obligation to interfere both in states and in nations within states, such as indigenous nations, to provide them with the benefits of their wisdom.

This is highly reminiscent of the process of colonialism, in which missionaries and others perceived their own actions as sanctified by a higher power. The connections with colonial modes of reform do not cease there. Neoliberalism has a rich connection with colonial attitudes of civilising indigenous peoples, even after their 'independence' from 'colonial rule'.

Connecting to colonisation: assumptions about peoples
Neoliberalism has a past and a history which is filled with particular kinds of attitudes towards indigenous peoples and indigenous cultures. These attitudes view indigenous peoples and cultures as obstacles to economic development which must be eliminated, or, more prevalent recently, as obstacles which can nonetheless acquire a greater level of civilisation through the right kind of training.

Recently in Aotearoa, these attitudes and assumptions have been extended somewhat, so that even with the level of training required by neoliberals, indigenous peoples are never ultimately allowed to exercise their sovereignty because the bar is always being raised higher and the rules keep changing.

Neoliberal advocates in the Pacific continue to perpetuate the spread of older ideas about degrees of civilisation and techniques of civilising, although now more covertly. While past colonisers were relatively open about their perceptions of indigenous peoples, neoliberal advocates in the Pacific now face the challenge that the 'savage people' with whom Captain Cook transacted now have their own independent states. Having been admitted to the system of states, Pacific countries now expect to be treated as equals rather than as 'savages'. Given this statehood, policies which were previously applied to indigenous peoples as subject populations must now be directed at them through the structures of the state.

Treating the former 'savage people' as supposed equals has meant that the neoliberals have diversified the tactics used for training and civilising indigenous peoples into allegedly 'technical' policies and 'adjustments' directed at their states. Neoliberalism demonstrates, therefore, a translation of many older colonial beliefs, once expressed explicitly, now expressed implicitly, into language and practices which are far more covert about their civilising mission.[40] Neoliberal advocates are also more firmly convinced that the market is the most important mechanism in the civilising process, without any overtly accompanying colonial endeavours or official colonies, but rather operating with people 'as if' they were the free and rational decision makers of independent states.[41]

This kind of neoliberal stance has particular consequences for Māori, who, despite not having an independent state as such, do experience similar pressures being directed at tribal governance entities, for example through the Crown-designed Treaty of Waitangi Settlement process, where corporate or corporate-type structures are strongly encouraged for tribes.

A key feature of neoliberal policies is this conflict between not wanting to be or appear paternalistic, wanting to be seen to allow people the 'freedom' and 'empowerment' to govern themselves, but at the same time distrusting the abilities of some peoples, particularly indigenous peoples, to do so. In order to deal in these new ways with indigenous peoples, two strategies have been adopted: first, emphasising the technical, economistic and 'rational' nature of neoliberal policies as more scientifically-based than other models; and secondly, more firmly tailoring the appearance and the rhetoric of neoliberal policies to the principles demanded by opponents of neoliberalism, which provides the appearance of empowering people through reconnecting the avowedly 'purely economic' policies with the more 'political' concerns related to governing. This could also be seen, however, as applying the rationale of 'economics' to areas and spheres which have previously operated in other ways.[42]

Since neoliberal policies are largely articulated as though they are founded on neutral, technical and scientific 'facts' derived from nature,[43] neoliberal advocates subsequently reject criticism of their policies by characterising it as non-rational, non-logical, non-neutral and non-scientific. One substantial justification for neoliberal policies is the claim that economic relations are to a significant extent natural. When conceived in this way, policies such as privatisation are not an imposition of one version of the world on another, akin to a process of re-colonisation, but are instead supposedly 'assisting in what is a natural course of development'.[44] The usage of the term 'rational' by neoliberals can be seen as 'a propaganda coup of the highest order... It carries the implication that any criticisms of it, or any alternatives put forward, are by definition irrational, and hence not worthy of serious contemplation'.[45]

A number of prominent neoliberal advocates do admit that their policies are artificially constructed, although, as they describe it, to be beneficial, not oppressive. Joseph Stiglitz, for example, argues that, 'true development entails a transformation of society'.[46] He argues that a transformation must take place to draw developing countries into the international economy, because it *could* be beneficial for them if they and 'developed' countries adopt the appropriate policies. This perspective is that which links the need for 'reform' of 'governance' to what are, for neoliberal advocates, merely technically conceived problems of economics. Stiglitz's argument recalls the older colonial desire to transform societies so that they are 'capable' of governing. These ideas seek to introduce institutions which will map over indigenous ones.

Resistance

The threat that neoliberal practices pose for indigenous ways of life, most importantly by extending the market mechanism to all areas of life previously governed in other ways, is the reason for much of Māori resistance. The extension of the market mechanism seeks to override the ways that Māori have previously thought about and governed their lives and resources. Neoliberal practices threaten Māori world-views, which understand the relationship between Māori and resources as diverse and holistic, rather than market based. For many Māori, if neoliberal ways of thinking cannot coexist alongside other world-views, but instead seek to dominate and colonise Māori world-views, then these practices must be resisted.

Resistance to neoliberal practices as a form of colonisation takes multiple forms, including attempts to decolonise, both by dismantling colonial structures and by supposedly purifying aspects of indigenous culture which are seen to have been contaminated by colonial practices. Linda Tuhiwai Smith argues that decolonisation is primarily a 'long-term process involving the bureaucratic, cultural, linguistic and psychological divesting of colonial power'.[47] From this perspective, decolonisation is ongoing resistance.

Decolonising is often seen as first requiring the dismantling of colonial infrastructure. Infrastructure may not always be physical; a 'decolonising of the mind'[48] is also seen as essential. Haunani-Kay Trask argues that:

> The first stage of resistance involves a throwing off, or a peeling apart of a forced way of behaving. Layers of engineered assimilation begin to come loose in the face of alternatives, *Native cultural alternatives*.[49]

Trask is describing what she sees as a dialectical process, in which the decolonising of the mind is aided by the reinvigoration of Native cultures and traditions.

The production of cultural identity in a self-determined sense, which confronts and complicates or instigates change from neoliberal agents, can be seen as successful resistance. Trask argues that, 'in the colonial context, all native cultural resistance is political: it challenges hegemony'.[50] While it seems difficult to see how native cultural resistance would not be political, it is important to add that native culture itself is political, and can challenge hegemony, but does not always do so. Cultural resistance, therefore, as the production of identity, becomes not something dislocated from the practices and effects of the political economy, but as simultaneously something restricted by it, as challenging it, and as disconnected from it.

Reasserting and strengthening particular cultural ways, that is, through the teaching and preservation of indigenous languages, philosophy, science, dances, artistic and ceremonial activities, is the second dimension of uncovering and recovering practices which in turn, because of their active difference, challenge the neoliberal form of world construction and force the neoliberal construction to negotiate a way around it. Often the reason for having to strengthen or reassert cultural ways is a consequence of colonisation, and is therefore reactive. This means that as an act, cultural reassertion is inextricable from this historical context, impinging and building on the present. This does not mean that cultural strengthening is merely, and therefore always, re-active, an act or acts of anti-colonial (or anti re-colonial) resistance. Sometimes cultural strengthening operates for more local, deontological or familial reasons. In this regard, cultural strengthening is about perceived commitments to maintaining the operation of, for example, communal land, sites of significance, language and concepts, for very practical purposes, such as continuing to be able to conduct tribal/community ceremonies. Cultural strengthening in this regard is located within a historical context, but is also highly pragmatic.

In an African context, Pal Ahluwalia has also argued that decolonisation 'cannot be equated with "after colonialism"'.[51] He argues that decolonisation is a process which involves the culture of both the colonisers and the colonised, and is essential to liberation and theories of resistance. He insists, however, that this form of decolonisation must also recognise 'cultural hybridity'[52] as an avenue through which to pursue forms of identity that do not merely reproduce the xenophobia and exclusionism of the older national liberation struggles.[53]

To bridge the impasse and move beyond a strict colonial versus anti-colonial/un-colonial binary, while continuing to acknowledge that neoliberal practices as a form of colonisation may be taking place, requires a broader understanding of resistance.

A broader conception of resistance

A broader conception of resistance could highlight the inextricable connection between formal/visible and deliberate acts of resistance (the traditional conception) and 'everyday acts of resistance'[54] or acts of 'making do'.[55] Both everyday acts and acts of 'making do' emphasise the daily and 'ordinary' practices of people as actively reshaping and actively participating in power relationships. Michel de Certeau uses the example of indigenous Indian cultures:

[E]ven when they were subjected, indeed even when they accepted their subjection, the Indians often used the laws, practices, and representations that were imposed on them by force or by fascination to ends other than those of their conquerors; they made something else out of them; they subverted them from within – not by rejecting them or by transforming them (though that occurred as well), but by many different ways of using them in the service of rules, customs or convictions foreign to the colonisation which they could not escape.[56]

Re-configuring anti-colonial resistance as including everyday acts and acts of 'making do' attempts to avoid the kinds of binary positions which produce an impasse between indigenous and non-indigenous peoples. A definition of resistance which emphasises these acts and strategies highlights that they are not merely practices in response to colonial practices, but exist beyond such a dichotomy; they are exercises of indigenous power. By highlighting strategies that overlap in different ways with colonialism, we can potentially achieve a wider picture of what takes place in Aotearoa, which includes practices normally obscured by an overemphasis on the dominating and 'all powerful' colonial/neoliberal machine.

In addition, by highlighting a multitude of Māori everyday acts of resistance and of 'making do', we can reconfigure these practices as more than stagnant, opportunistic acts of 'invented tradition'. Viewing these acts in this way helps to reconfigure indigenous traditions as more than stagnant and rigidified practices with no 'modern' relevance, rather as everyday negotiations, dynamic and changing cultural practices.

In this book, a broad definition of resistance is used that attempts to encourage consideration of the diversity of Māori resistance. Broader definitions of resistance highlight both overt resistance acts and the implicit daily challenges to neoliberal practices that exist in Māori lives and world-views.

This book is divided into four parts. The chapters in Part One outline the context of neoliberalism in Aotearoa, and detail a range of effects on Māori. This includes the impact neoliberal practices have had on the Treaty settlements process, and an examination of practices underpinning the New Zealand health system that may compound the negative effects of neoliberalism on Māori. Part Two presents chapters that emphasise Māori world-views and the use of Māori stories and tikanga as challenges to neoliberal practices. Part Three gives candid interviews with two activists who are negotiating complex roles and struggling to untangle neoliberal practices in their own work and lives. The chapters in Part Four explore Māori resisting forced inclusion in international economic frameworks, while simultaneously using international human rights frameworks to create connections and draw support from other indigenous peoples.

No book can cover everything, and this book makes no claim to cover all aspects and features of neoliberal policies and practices, or every angle of Māori resistance to them. It does, however, present a range of counter-views to challenge the neoliberal insistence that theirs is the only world in existence. It is a beginning.

Notes

1 In their article, John Gallagher and Ronald Robinson argue that 'free' trade was a British policy which did not cover just a singular activity, but rather was conjoined with 'informal control if possible; trade with rule when necessary'. J. Gallagher and R. Robinson, 'The Imperialism of Free Trade', *The Economic History Review*, Vol. 6, No. 1, 1953, p. 13.

2 For further analysis on this point, see P. Ormerod, *The Death of Economics*, London: Faber and Faber, 1994, p. 17; A. Engler, *Apostles of Greed: Capitalism and the Myth of the Individual in the Market*, London: Pluto Press, 1995, p. 131.

3 Ormerod, 1994, p. 17.

4 For a discussion of the expansion of financial markets in the early 1900s, see J. M. Keynes, *The General Theory of Employment Interest and Money*, London: Macmillan, [1936] 1964.

5 For further analysis on this point, see D. Korten, *The Post-corporate World: Life After Capitalism*, Sydney: Pluto Press, 2000, p. 49.

6 There is a further diversity among these categories, such as long and short term distinctions, but an exploration of these distinctions is not essential to the argument here.

7 See, for example, J. McMaster, 'Strategies to Stimulate Private Sector Development in the Pacific Island Economies', in R. Cole and S. Tambunlertchai (eds), *The Future of Asia-Pacific Economies: Pacific Islands at the Crossroads?* Canberra: National Centre for Development Studies, The Australian National University, 1993.

8 United Nations Conference on Trade and Development, *FDI in Developing Countries At A Glance*, Geneva: United Nations, 2001, p. iv.

9 United Nations Development Programme, *Human Development Report: Globalization with a Human Face*, Oxford: Oxford University Press, 1999a, p. 2.

10   See T. Marjoram, 'Technology Transfer', in T. Marjoram (ed.), *Island Technology: Technology for Development in the South Pacific,* London: Intermediate Technology Publications, 1994.

11   M. Khor, 'Global Economy and the Third World', in J. Mander and E. Goldsmith (eds), *The Case Against the Global Economy and For a Turn Toward the Local*. San Francisco: Sierra Club Books, 1996, p.49.

12   IMF, 'Statutory Purposes' and 'Articles of Agreement of the International Monetary Fund, Article I, Purposes', IMF website, http://www.imf.org (accessed 14/10/2002).

13   See, for example, comments made by IMF Managing Director, Horst Köhler, at a meeting with civil society representatives in 2002. IMF website, http://www.imf.org/external/np/tr/2002/tr020117a.htm (accessed 9/11/2004).

14   R. Barnet and J. Cavanagh, 'Electronic Money and the Casino Economy', in Mander and Goldsmith, 1996.

15   B. Warf, 'Telecommunications and Economic Space', in E. Sheppard and T. J. Barnes, *A Companion to Economic Geography*, Oxford: Blackwell, 2000, p. 487.

16   Korten, 2000, p. 51.

17   See also P. Bourdieu, 'Utopia of Endless Exploitation', *Le Monde Diplomatique*, December 1998, www.monde-diplomatique.fr/en/1998/12/08bourdieu.html (accessed 15/10/2002). For a critique of the mechanistic nature of neoliberal analysis, see W. J. Samuels (ed.), *Economics as Discourse: An Analysis of the Language of Economics*, Boston: Kluwer Academic Publishers, 1990.

18   For some liberals, the state was seen as able to play a productive role in the regulation of certain activities and in the process of supporting economic growth. John Maynard Keynes, for example, whose conception of the state is often criticised by neoliberals, argued that the state had an important responsibility in organising investment, as the fluctuations of the market need to be offset. Keynes, [1936] 1964, p. 164.

19   C. Waligorski, *The Political Theory of Conservative Economists*, Kansas: University Press of Kansas, 1990, p. 168.

20   M. Otter, 'Privatisation: an Agenda for the South Pacific', in *Pacific Economic Bulletin*, Vol. 9, No.1, 1994, p. 35.

21   B. Knapman and C. D. Saldanha, *Reforms in the Pacific,* Manila: Asian Development Bank, 1999, p. 170.

22   World Bank, *Pacific Islands Regional Economic Report: Embarking on a Global Voyage: Trade Liberalization and Complementary Reforms in the Pacific*, Poverty Reduction and Economic Management Unit, East Asia and Pacific Region, 2002.

23   F. Hayek, *The Fatal Conceit: The Errors of Socialism,* London: Routledge, 1988, p. 6.

24   A. Smith, *An Inquiry Into The Nature And Causes of The Wealth of Nations*, Edinburgh: Adam and Charles Black, [1776] 1872.

25   Ormerod, 1994, p. 41.

26   Ibid, p.45. It was this small and particular part of Smith's analysis, regarding the 'invisible hand' guiding the mechanisms of the market, which was translated into mathematics in the 'marginal revolution' by Leon Walras and William Jevons, and has been highlighted as evidence of the natural function of markets. Regarding this point, Paul Ormerod and Michael Shapiro argue that this version of Smith and his work fails to adequately reflect the emphasis he placed on moral issues, which he saw as crucial to discussions of economics. M. J. Shapiro, *Reading 'Adam Smith': Desire, History and Value*, London: Sage Publications, 1993.

27   Waligorski, 1990, p. 35.

28   M. Friedman, *Capitalism and Freedom,* Chicago: The University of Chicago Press, 1962, p. 12.

29   Waligorski, 1990, p. 68.

30   Ibid, p. 55.

31   See F. M. Lappé and J. Collins, *World Hunger: 12 Myths,* London: Earthscan, 1998, p. 99-100; Engler, 1995, p. 50; Waligorski, 1990, p. 25.

32   Friedman, 1962, p. 13.

33   Ibid, p. 15.

34   Ormerod, 1995, p. 27.

35 One strong indication of the failure of GDP as an adequate measure of real changes in standards of living is the situation in Papua New Guinea. As a consultant for the ADB points out, 'Despite a GDP per head higher than several of its neighbors, at around $1,250, PNG's human development indicators are the worst in the Pacific.' Despite having been widely criticised, GDP continues to be used to assess the progress of peoples, nations and states. See A. V. Hughes, *A Different Kind of Voyage: Development and Dependence in the Pacific Islands,* Manila: Office of Pacific Operations, Asian Development Bank, 1998, pp. 21, 45.

36 M. Chossudovsky, *The Globalisation of Poverty,* Philippines: Institute of Political Economy, 1997.

37 World Bank website: www.worldbank.org

38 As Christina Rojas has shown, when the poor become the 'true poverty experts', while this may provide them with some capacity to determine policies which govern them, simultaneously they become responsible for getting 'out' of or remaining 'in' poverty. C. Rojas, 'Governing Through the Social: the Role of International Financial Institutions in the Third World', paper presented at the International Studies Association meeting, Chicago, 21 February 2001.

39 See, for example, United Nations, *World Economic and Social Survey,* New York: Department of Economic and Social Information and Policy Analysis, United Nations, 2000.

40 B. Hindess, 'Neo-liberal Citizenship', *Citizenship Studies,* Vol. 6, No. 2, 2002, p. 9.

41 For discussions of how people are governed through their own choices as 'free' individuals, but not specifically in the context of independent states, see Barry et al., 1996.

42 B. Hindess, 'A Society Governed by Contract?' in G. Davis, B. Sullivan and A. Yeatman, *The New Contractualism,* Brisbane: Centre for Australia Public Sector Management, 1997, p. 22. Also see G. Burchell, 'Liberal Government and Techniques of the Self', in A. Barry, T. Osborne and N. Rose, *Foucault and Political Reason,* Chicago: University of Chicago Press, 1996.

43 Ibid. Graham Burchell has argued that neoliberals admit the market is not natural, but rather can only exist under certain political, legal and institutional conditions.

44 D. Williams, 'Constructing the Economic Space: The World Bank and the Making of Homo Oeconomicus', *Millennium: Journal of International Studies,* Vol. 28, No.1, 1999, p. 81.

45 Ormerod, 1994, pp. 111–112.

46 J. Stiglitz, 'Trade and the Developing World: A New Agenda', *Current History,* November 1999, p. 389.

47 L. T. Smith, *Decolonizing Methodologies,* Dunedin: University of Otago Press, 1999, p. 98.

48 N. wa Thiong'o, *Decolonising the Mind: The Politics of Language in African Literature,* London: James Currey, 1981.

49 H. K. Trask, *From a Native Daughter: Colonialism and Sovereignty in Hawai'I,* Maine: Common Courage Press, 1993, p. 115.

50 Ibid, p. 54.

51 P. Ahluwalia, *Politics and Post-colonial Theory: African Inflections,* London: Routledge, 2001, p. 50.

52 Ibid, p. 51.

53 Ibid, pp. 50–51.

54 J. C. Scott, *Weapons of the Weak,* New Haven: Yale University Press, 1985.

55 M. de Certeau, *The Practice of Everyday Life,* Berkeley: University of California Press, 1984, p. 29.

56 Ibid, pp. 31–32.

Part One

Part One explores the context of neoliberalism in Aotearoa and how it has impacted on Māori. Maria Bargh examines the way that neoliberal practices have been interlaced with the Crown's Treaty of Waitangi settlements process, and how this has encouraged the commodification of tribal structures and relationships. Bridget Robson highlights a range of trends in Māori health that suggest critical reflection is required on how colonial values, underpinning the health system, may be contributing to the worsening of Māori health and may be exacerbated by neoliberal policies and practices. These chapters emphasise the neoliberal context in Aotearoa, and provide a framework for the diverse challenges and acts of resistance covered in Parts Two, Three and Four.

Chapter 1
Maria Bargh – Māori Development and Neoliberalism

Chapter 2
Bridget Robson – Economic Determinants of Māori Health and Disparities

1

Māori Development and Neoliberalism

Maria Bargh

Once called 'Chile without the gun',[1] Aotearoa is one of the world leaders of neoliberalism.[2] Successive New Zealand governments since 1984 have pursued neoliberal policies with a faith, vehemence and confidence in their success that few other governments appear to possess. In this way, Aotearoa can be seen as having gone further with neoliberal policies than many other countries. To varying degrees, those same governments have been keen, as are Māori, to progress the settlement of Māori claims against the Crown[3] for breaches of Te Tiriti o Waitangi (Te Tiriti)[4] – both historical and recent.

In this chapter I discuss the impact of neoliberal policies on Māori in this context. I suggest that the neoliberal agenda of successive governments permeates the settlements process, resulting in the separation and neglect of various intrinsic issues, such as constitutional change and commodification of process.

The settlements process is at the heart of the debate. A central understanding of both the Crown and Māori is that a prerequisite for Māori development is the resolution of particular policies of colonialism, most specifically the return of land deemed to have been wrongfully taken, and the redress of other breaches of Te Tiriti o Waitangi. Although Māori have been demanding solutions to such breaches since Te Tiriti was first signed in 1840, the implementation of the settlements process since 1984 provides an excellent example of aspects of indigenous resistance to a concerted neoliberal programme.

This chapter describes the settlements process in detail, and explores the neoliberal assumptions and boundaries that form the basic structure of the settlements process, namely the commodification of Māori claims and rights, and the corporatisation of the structure of the tribe.

The Crown has embedded the neoliberal agenda firmly into the settlements process. Promoted as a 'full and final' resolution of grievances, the Crown claims this is an opportunity for 'long-term economic benefits for Māori'.[5] The separation of Treaty settlements from broader Treaty issues of sovereignty and power sharing suggests that the Crown is attempting to ignore issues of shared sovereignty and constitutional change.

Before examining the legacies stemming from the Treaty of Waitangi, a few preliminary explanations may be in order. The Treaty of Waitangi, signed between the British Crown and Māori in 1840, exists in two versions, which continue to produce significant deviations on how to understand which rights are guaranteed and what behaviour is appropriate for both parties. The two versions are in English and Māori, and are known as the Treaty of Waitangi and Te Tiriti o Waitangi respectively. Most Māori signed the Māori version.[6]

It is not my intention here to provide an exhaustive account of the significance of the versions; however, three points are pertinent to my later discussion. First, it is commonly understood that the Crown's relationship with Māori must be based on Te Tiriti o Waitangi. In 1987, in the case of *New Zealand Māori Council v Attorney-General*, the Appeal Court found that the Crown is required to actively protect the interests of Māori. While the English version of the Treaty states that Māori ceded 'sovereignty', the Māori version uses the word 'kawanatanga', government, to refer to the rights conferred upon the Crown, rather than 'tino rangatiratanga', sovereignty, which is reaffirmed to Māori.[7]

From the beginning, this meant that there were vastly different interpretations of what Te Tiriti meant, most importantly whether it was merely between two parties, or between equal nations, particularly given the signing of the Declaration of Independence prior to Te Tiriti in 1835.[8] It can be argued that many Māori understood it to be the latter, while the Crown has largely favoured the former. For Māori, therefore, the achievement and maintenance of tino rangatiratanga as nations within New Zealand has long been a central goal, which is now often articulated as being broadly synonymous with Māori development.[9]

The settlements process
Māori have continually argued, protested and lobbied for the correction of injustices, restitution, and the return of land and other resources taken during colonisation. The Treaty settlements process for most Māori is therefore premised upon notions of justice and redress. In this regard, the form that the settlements process takes, and not merely the end result, is of central significance.

Paul McHugh argues that there is a divergence, however, between the way that the settlements process is viewed by Māori and by Pākehā, or the Crown. He argues that the 'Māori discourse is highly historicised, the Anglo-settler one is calculatedly dehistoricised'.[10] McHugh argues that the Crown's neoliberal position fits appropriately with this dehistoricisation, as settlements are most importantly emphasised as final, much like a contract. There is a perception, he argues, that once the settlement contract has been completed, then the past is to be forgotten.[11] As McHugh argues elsewhere, the settlements completed with the Crown to date have not appeared to be particularly concerned with establishing mechanisms by which a relationship between Crown and tribes can be extended beyond the settlement itself. Rather, 'Their purpose has been to settle or silence the claim; their goal has been the quietening of complaint rather than the discovery of a mechanism for continual dialogue.'[12] For example, the extended preamble in the Tainui tribe's settlement outlining Te Tiriti breaches against Tainui was more significant for Tainui as recognition of historical injustices that continue to be relevant in the present. However, for the Crown these were peripheral, placed outside the actual text of the document, and of secondary relevance to the finality of the agreement and the past. While McHugh's argument can be understood in light of the way that many of the Deeds of Settlement have been written,[13] the Crown has demonstrated some level of understanding of the importance for Māori of having Te Tiriti breaches investigated by agreeing to the establishment and continued funding of the Waitangi Tribunal.

The establishment of the Waitangi Tribunal in 1975 was a watershed in the settlements process. The Tribunal was established to 'inquire into and make findings upon a claim and, if it decided the claim was well founded, to recommend to Government measures to redress'.[14] Initially, the Tribunal could hear claims relating only to events that had occurred since 1975. In 1985, the Waitangi Tribunal Act was amended to include claims relating to events since 1840. For the Labour Government at the time, the Waitangi Tribunal seemed to be an appropriate avenue to placate Māori in a politically and economically inexpensive way. As W. H. Oliver observes, 'It was not expected to hear many claims, to meet often or to cost much.'[15] This proved seriously incorrect, as shown by the consequences of several Waitangi Tribunal findings and recommendations, which are detailed below. One consequence has been that nearly the entire operation of the Native Land Court, established in the 1860s to create individual title to communally owned Māori lands so that they could be sold, was found to be contrary to Te Tiriti.[16]

It has been the Tribunal that has been at the nexus of the interplay between neoliberal policies, greater Māori autonomy, and transfers of 'assets' to Māori. As Paul Joseph has argued, the Tribunal's work has evolved in the:

> midst of a collision between two contradictory forces: on the one hand, a genuine political will to improve the situation for Māori; on the other, a new commitment to neo-liberal economic policies that transformed state structures and undermined the capacity to fulfil the promises generated by that political will.[17]

Despite being placed in this potentially conflicting position, the Tribunal has continued to be viewed and used by Māori as an avenue to have historical injustices investigated and redressed, as evidenced by the continual registering of new cases. In this sense, we can understand that many Māori view the function of the Tribunal as one of historical and societal significance.

The Tribunal reports have also contributed significantly to a systematic documentation of Te Tiriti breaches and to greater legitimation of redress and compensation. In addition, the Tribunal has not been constrained to historical investigation only, but has allowed investigation into present and future rights, such as those relating to minerals and future technologies. Tribunal reports have often been critical of Crown actions. The Tribunal has even acknowledged the commodifying nature of the Crown's neoliberal policies. [18] In the *Muriwhenua Report*, the Tribunal highlighted the discrepancies between the kinds of values enshrined in Te Tiriti, and those enshrined in such policies.[19] The Tribunal argued not only that the fisheries quota management system, established by the Crown, was fundamentally in breach of Te Tiriti, but also that 'fishing has become corporatised. The Government has issued shares in a resource that was once seen as publicly owned ... it has created a property interest in the right to harvest.'[20]

This perception of the role of the Tribunal as an activist one diverges from Crown intentions for it to be merely a pacification mechanism and a facilitator for finalising agreements. Recent governments have become impatient with the speed with which the Tribunal is investigating and reporting on cases, in line with general Pākehā public opinion.[21] This has led to recent governments expanding the significance placed on the work of the Office of Treaty Settlements (OTS) and encouraging Māori to enter into direct negotiations with the Crown, thus sidelining the Tribunal.

One of the most insightful cases involving the Tribunal in the nexus between Māori and the neoliberal agenda, came as the fourth Labour Government sought to implement the reforms of the 1980s. As a vital cornerstone for the government's neoliberal agenda, the State Owned Enterprises (SOE) Act 1986 sought to corporatise and privatise state-owned assets. However, many state-owned enterprises owned lands that were subject to Māori claims through the Waitangi Tribunal, or lands that Māori could have intentions of claiming in the future.

The New Zealand Māori Council took the Crown to court, highlighting section 9 of the SOE Act, which states that 'Nothing in this Act shall permit the Crown to act in a manner that is inconsistent with the principles of the Treaty of Waitangi.'[22] In the ensuing case, the Court of Appeal ruled that the principles of Te Tiriti included protecting from alienation land that was subject to claim under the Tribunal.[23] As a result, the Court of Appeal found the Act to be unlawful in breaching the principles of Te Tiriti. The case was settled by Parliament enacting the Treaty of Waitangi (State Enterprises) Act 1988, which required that all Crown land being sold was required to carry memorials when privatised, meaning that the land could be returned to the Crown and subsequently to Māori if a claim was proven. The decision set the important precedent that 'the duty of the Crown is not merely passive, but extends to active protection of Māori people in the use of their land and waters to the fullest extent possible'.[24]

This decision was a far cry from the 1877 judgement of Judge Prendergast, who ruled that the Treaty was a simple nullity.[25] It was also an important indication, not merely that perceptions of Te Tiriti and the potential scope of settlements and Māori development had changed, but also that there had been a shift in thinking around the Crown's Te Tiriti obligations. The Foreshore and Seabed Act 2004 and subsequent Labour Government actions, however, can be seen as a recent return to pre-1900 modes of Crown thinking regarding Māori rights.

Sections 9 and 27 of the SOE Act were enacted in such a hurried way that, it has been argued, the Labour Government in fact conceded much more than it would have done under ordinary circumstances. As Jane Kelsey writes:

> (g)iven the urgency there was little opportunity for a detailed scrutiny of the two clauses by other officials or consultation

with Māori. Neither Cabinet nor caucus was involved ... Indeed it is quite possible that the clauses would not have survived the normal vetting processes.[26]

Thus, the legal action taken by the New Zealand Māori Council ensured that aspects of Te Tiriti were incorporated into laws, and the courts were enabled to make rulings on them. Ironically, this change, which had significant benefits for Māori, emerged out of hasty legislative change, a tactic often used by successive governments to hurry neoliberal policies through Parliament without public consultation.

The case of *New Zealand Māori Council v Attorney-General* may have highlighted to the Crown that if the settlements process proceeded through the courts and in an ad hoc fashion, this could be financially disastrous. A more formalised process could be more expedient. Therefore, the initiation of the settlements process was, in a sense, a Crown concession forced by Māori. Some Māori interpreted the Labour Government's moves as a 'damage control strategy to neutralise court imposed legal settlements'.[27] As Alan Ward observes, 'The Māori demand for justice in terms of the Treaty was overwhelming, and Parliament could not turn its back.'[28]

More importantly, however, when the National Government resumed the settlements process in the early 1990s, the country was feeling the effects of extreme neoliberal policies. Unemployment had risen significantly, particularly among Māori, leading to increased numbers of people receiving government assistance. Between 1989 and 1990, the total number of people receiving the unemployment benefit increased by 20 per cent.[29] At the same time there was a drive to cut the amount of revenue spent on government benefits. These realities, combined with the National Government's equally neoliberal approach, including its deliberate and determined campaign attacking 'welfare dependency', led to generally increased animosity towards those perceived as illegitimately dependent on 'taxpayers', and particularly towards Māori beneficiaries. They also undoubtedly increased racist attitudes within Aotearoa, in terms of stereotyping Māori as 'lazy dole bludgers' and 'irresponsible sole parents', who were 'draining the hard earned resources of others'.[30]

In 1994, in an attempt to place limits on Treaty settlements, Māori were offered a settlement package that became known as the Fiscal Envelope.[31] The Crown's proposal stated that a limited sum of one billion dollars was being made available for the settlement of all Māori claims. The proposal sought to clarify who could bring claims to the Waitangi Tribunal, to restrict the types of claims that could be made, and to finalise the preliminary boundaries for negotiation. The proposal also outlined particular kinds of governance structures that were to be required before the transfer of assets could take place.[32]

Essentially, the Fiscal Envelope proposals sought to limit and govern Māori claims and future structures in forms and ways determined by and expedient for the Crown. At meetings called by the Crown and Māori, the proposal was rejected outright by tribes throughout the country.[33] Not only was the sum perceived by many Māori to be astonishingly low, but no formula was provided as to how the sum had been determined, and many assumed it was merely arbitrary. Alan Ward makes the point that if all Māori claimants argued for 'just compensation', in the legal sense of the value of the asset cost plus compound interest, the figure of one billion dollars is indeed ridiculously low.[34]

Moreover, the way in which the Crown claimed to be seeking consultation, while making it clear that much of the offer was non-negotiable, was widely resented. This was contrary to the forms of consultation laid down in the Waitangi Tribunal *Manukau Report*, in which the Tribunal noted that 'A failure to consult may be seen as an affront to the standing of indigenous tribes.'[35]

In response to the Fiscal Envelope and the Crown's separation within it of broad Te Tiriti responsibilities and implications from the settlements, participants at the 1995 Hirangi meeting in Turangi attempted to reconnect the issues.[36] They proposed various models for constitutional change, including a senate, regional representation, and separate governments. In reply, the

National Government 'rejected the suggestion that the settlement process was in any way a constitutional matter'.[37] This once more enabled the Crown to limit the potential avenues and scope for settlements, as well as future Māori development.

Separation for commodification

Not only is the historical nature of the settlements process important for Māori development, so too is the potential for further future political development through constitutional change. This aim conflicts sharply with successive governments' ideas about limiting the potential scope of settlements, and the potential scope of tino rangatiratanga as a component of Māori development.

A key strategy of the Treaty settlements process has been to allow negotiation on only that narrow range of issues that the Crown has deemed acceptable. There has been a separation of the settlements process from broader Te Tiriti issues, such as constitutional change. This parallels the neoliberal strategy of claiming to remove the political from the economic, while increasingly applying the economic to areas previously governed in other ways. Such separations inherently favour the Crown position, and allow Māori only limited scope to actually achieve what they consider important. Even Treasury noted in 1988 that 'Māoridom is often distrustful of the separation of social and economic goals.'[38] Māori have sought to resist such a separation of the issues, continually reasserting that broad Te Tiriti issues must always be contextualised and examined holistically.

To counteract the kind of skewing of the debate presented by the Crown, members of the Tino Rangatiratanga Māori Independence movement have responded by highlighting the normative level of the debate and persisted in calling for negotiations to be placed in a framework of justice and rights.[39] Moana Jackson argues that:

> Any agreement that sees financial return as the equivalent of rangatiratanga, or that accepts as its values-base the belief that profit is the same as redress for colonisation, will not be full and final – and it will sadly cause division and discontent.[40]

Jackson argues that issues surrounding Te Tiriti and rights derived from it must always be located in the political as well as the economic context, as they come from a process of colonisation, of dispossession of one people, land, culture and law by another. 'The attempt to isolate the Treaty of Waitangi from that political reality is to remove it from its truth. It is to confine Māori people forever to that limbo, somewhere between laughter and tears.'[41] Jackson's argument relocates the legacy of colonialism as centrally important, overriding commodity concerns alone.

The New Zealand Law Commission has, at times, supported an understanding of the settlement process as more holistic. In their report on *Māori Custom and Values in New Zealand Law*, they stated:

> If society is truly to give effect to the promise of the Treaty of Waitangi to provide a secure place for Māori values within New Zealand society, then the commitment must be total. It must involve a real endeavour to understand what tikanga Māori is, how it is practised and applied and how integral it is to the social, economic, cultural and political development of Māori still encapsulated within a dominant culture in New Zealand society.[42]

What they appear to be arguing for here is not merely an incorporation of the broader political and constitutional implications with the economic ones, but for Māori culture to be seen *on its own terms*.[43] Actually doing so may be more productive in achieving lasting settlements if people feel that Te Tiriti breaches have been accorded greater recognition and resolution.

Commodification and affordability

Once a large part of the settlements process became defined by the Crown in commodified terms, the essence of the process shifted from Te Tiriti breaches and violation of rights to the transfer and management of capital assets and the redistribution of the dividends acquired from this capital. Quite different sets of possibilities and solutions for Māori development stem from each of these definitions of the settlements process. As was outlined in the Fiscal Envelope proposal, under the second definition, the issue becomes merely one of price and affordability.

As Ian Macduff points out, the 'debate' surrounding the Fiscal Envelope became one of bargaining over differing solutions, one of which would be pursued until a 'better' alternative was suggested. He argues that this is:

> a familiar pattern of the kind of bargaining where all that is at stake is an eventual agreement on price and each knows by some kind of convention that the 'right' price is somewhere less than is demanded and more than is offered. But that kind of bargaining does not readily carry over into the negotiation setting where something more than a commodity is at stake.[44]

Macduff highlights here the very distinction that the Crown is attempting to conceal: that they are quite strategically offering merely commodities in place of actual rights for Māori. As Macduff argues, this has clear implications for how the process of 'negotiation' takes place, as it is itself a cultural activity; in this case, it was offered as non-negotiable. He suggests that as the negotiation is designed to be one concerning commodities, it becomes acceptable, according to the Crown, to negotiate as one would regarding commodities. We can surmise, however, that if the debate were redesigned to take into account the entire ensemble of Te Tiriti breaches, including constitutional change, as argued by Tino Rangatiratanga advocates, then the process would be required to be more democratic, consultative and slow.

Corporate warriors

The Crown is not alone in encouraging the commodification of the settlements process. The significance of corporate warriors in this regard should not be neglected. The term 'corporate warriors' has been coined to refer to Māori who claim that the economic development of their iwi (tribe) is the most important component that will lead to greater social and political development. The corporate warrior perspective claims to be attempting to combine a social and an economic position. Corporate warriors believe that Māori involvement in business can support social ends, without being solely about profit, thus attempting to establish some form of middle ground between ethics and business. Some have argued that this fusion of the social back into business ethics means that the presence of Māori business provides a new perspective from which 'dominant ethics of the Western order can be questioned'.[45]

Corporate warriors often agree on a neoliberal avenue for the achievement of social ends, at times articulating these views in terms of Māori self-determination and independence. Donna Awatere-Huata, a prominent former member of the extreme neoliberal party ACT, has perhaps best demonstrated the way that neoliberalism can co-opt or simply use a discourse of self-determination. She argues that she sees rangatiratanga as 'the right to do your own thing, the right to determine your own destiny. Not to have bureaucrats making those decisions for you.'[46] By positioning the option of 'bureaucrats doing it' on one side, and 'doing it yourself' on the other, she sets up a narrow binary which implies that relationships based on independence and free choice are superior to regulation. In addition, she casts the discussion as one of rangatiratanga, linking the possibility of achieving Māori self-determination with neoliberal concepts of self-help.

Former Minister of Māori Affairs, Tau Henare, extended such a concept of neoliberal principles to apply potentially to all indigenous peoples. He argues that business is 'a primary medium through which indigenous peoples can achieve some sense of self-determination over their social and economic outcomes'.[47] The inadequacy of this view can be demonstrated by examining the greater complexity of particular forms of businesses which incorporate cultural values and practices that are potentially contrary to neoliberal ones.

Awatere's comments also link the notion of self-determination with neoliberal devolution. Decentralising the state and shifting service delivery to the private sector is a key neoliberal strategy. Articulating self-determination as self-management reduces it to an issue of service delivery by Māori, rather than actual policy formulation or decision making by Māori. The argument that Māori should provide services to Māori, which has been picked up by some Māori, facilitates the state's promotion of neoliberal policies to Māori as if they were about wider issues.

The fourth Labour Government's plans to shift responsibility for service delivery were often taken up with enthusiasm by Māori, when translated into what appeared to be an extension and facilitation of Māori control. In 1984, the Labour Government organised a Hui Taumata to discuss Māori needs and priorities. As Roger Maaka argues:

> The call from the conference was quite clear: Māori people wanted to break the dependency cycle of Government welfare schemes and have control over their own destiny. As it happened, this call for autonomy gelled with the free-market policies – 'Rogernomics' – espoused by then Minister of Finance Roger Douglas.[48]

In this way, many Māori unwittingly accommodated neoliberal policies because they linked them with the aim of achieving tino rangatiratanga. The 2005 Hui Taumata followed a similar framework, with many key speakers from the Labour Party presenting ideas about the need for Māori to make further use of corporate structures.[49]

Presenting the settlements merely in commodified terms constructs Māori claims as demands, which are somehow caught up in a neoliberal binary of needs and wants, so that whatever is not a need must be a want. This makes Māori claims appear unreasonable, selfish, and pursued merely for commercial gain. It is here that the structure of the institution that receives the settlement becomes crucial to determining how these resources will be managed for future generations.

Corporatising the tribe

Several commentators have noted that Māori are not merely individual citizens of the state, but possess a dual identity not available to other New Zealanders.[50] It is for this reason that neoliberal advocates must pay so much attention to the structure of the tribe, because it governs that part of Māori and Māori identity that is not directly or easily governable through the state apparatus. Māori are, therefore, under pressure to be ruled both as citizens and as tribal members.

Throughout the settlements process, the tribe itself has held dual personalities. Not only is it the entity that is the contracting party to Te Tiriti, and therefore, the central entity with which the Crown should be negotiating and settling;[51] but it is also perceived by the Crown and by many Māori as the central agent to facilitate Māori development, economically and culturally. Both these personalities of the tribe have been challenged, and both the Crown and different Māori groups have sought actively to shape the structure of the tribe, often in conflicting ways.

Others conceptualise the identity of the tribe as a nation, equal to the Crown, with the continued possession of tino rangatiratanga at the forefront of their idea about how the tribe should assist in Māori development. McHugh argues that 'tino rangatiratanga clearly involves Māori control of Māori assets and resources'.[52]

There have been various attempts by the Crown to regulate and govern the form of the tribe since Te Tiriti. However, my interest here is more specifically the way that the neoliberal policies of governing have contributed to the corporatisation of the tribe, that is, the way that principles of the market are being applied and incorporated within the structure of the tribe.[53]

New roles for the tribe

The Labour Government's neoliberal plans for the devolution of the services of the Department of Māori Affairs between 1984 and 1990, and subsequent roles of tribal organisations as service providers, placed new burdens and roles on those tribal organisations. Initially, it appeared that the state was giving more power to iwi, in line with Māori demands for control over resources. Many Māori perceived these moves as providing them with greater opportunities for the development of '"Māori solutions to Māori problems", thus enhancing tino rangatiratanga at the local level'.[54] In reality, what devolution meant for Māori, and for iwi in particular, was:

> a taking over, on a voluntary basis, of work that had been done by the Government departments funded by taxpayers. The theory was that Māori communities could handle Māori problems on their own and the under-resourced groups could implement social policy.[55]

This devolution occurred throughout the country, not just to Māori.[56] However, in the case of Māori, it was the tribe that was essentially left as the organisation to play this role of facilitator or service provider.

One of the Crown's prerequisites before a settlement agreement is signed is that iwi must restructure the organisation which will receive and administer the settlement. In *Crown Proposals for the Settlement of Treaty Claims*, the Crown claimed that it wished to be sure that the assets and resources transferred to Māori were 'managed and administered within a proper legal structure'.[57] This kind of structure includes forms of accounting and representation that the Crown deems acceptable.[58] The Crown does not directly insist on a particular model for this restructuring; however, there are other ways of manipulating this process by encouraging a particular mode of 'good governance' through the direct negotiation process with claimants. Anecdotal evidence suggests that the Office of Treaty Settlements establishes particular guidelines during negotiations that are non-negotiable. This creates new relations of power and regulation.

The Fisheries Commission (Te Ohu Kaimoana), which resulted from a pan-Māori settlement with the Crown regarding fisheries, has been instrumental in the perpetuation of a corporate structure for the tribe. Te Ohu Kaimoana has identified 'fundamental principles of organisation and governance relationships that iwi must comply with, in order to receive fisheries assets'.[59] If iwi do not comply, they will not receive their portion of the settlement. Te Ohu Kaimoana insists that iwi registers should be established to account for tribal members. While such registers, at one level, may be productive in reconnecting Māori with the tribe, this move fundamentally restructures Māori identity, through a separate organisation redefining the tribe and the relationship Māori can have with it. The effects are, as yet, unclear. With the introduction of iwi registers, many Māori who are unaware of their tribal connections risk losing the ability to earn or be part of their tribe, despite the fact that they should have access. For young, urban Māori who are out of communication with their traditional tribe, but who participate within pan–Māori urban authorities, the risks are also significant.

These changes have modified the form of the actual iwi organisation, but perhaps more importantly, they have also changed the relationship that members of the tribe have with it. The relationship has shifted from communitarian conceptions or interaction towards contractual relations between individuals and agencies. The concept of iwi is a cornerstone of the very way that Māori interact to support their turangawaewae[60] and other cultural values. By corporatising iwi, Māori can expect to experience radical changes in the way that such an organisation survives, and how people relate to and with it.

Tipene O'Regan has argued that the best form for the tribe is one in which tribal members are seen as 'shareholders', who are allocated dividends accruing to them in the form of a voucher.[61] They are then able to choose to redeem their voucher either for cash or for a share in the company/tribe. O'Regan argues that 'By this mechanism (or something like it) individuals, families or groups of kin could build their own personal stake and hold assets in their own right.'[62] This kind of structure places a large emphasis on property and returns, and on the choices of individuals, even though these may be made in relation to other individuals.

O'Regan's corporate version of the tribe demonstrates a significantly different kind of relationship among tribal members from the one outlined by Eddie Durie. Durie argues that tribal relations in the past, which have relevance to the current situation, were more concerned with relationships than with property. The 'common feature ... of Māori law was that it was not in fact about property, but about arranging relationships between people'.[63] Furthermore, he argues that the 'standard contract was [one of] gift, with the expectation of a return in due course. The purpose was to establish a permanent and personal relationship with reciprocal obligations where the main benefit to both sides would come in the course of time.'[64] While Durie's explanation primarily concerns tribes in the nineteenth century, many of these concepts continue to have relevance to and to be seen in the modern context, in tribal activities and on marae.[65] Durie is also referring to relations between different tribes; however, these kinds of concepts have similar implications within the tribe itself, and are significantly different from those espoused by O'Regan. This highlights the particular ways in which O'Regan's version of the tribe is a corporate one, primarily concerned with property and profit and the distribution of profit to individuals. Despite O'Regan's attempt to demonstrate how a tribal and corporate structure are successfully merged, the fundamental differences remain. Relationships and genealogy remain of utmost importance for many tribal member interactions, while corporate structures tend on the whole to create instrumental relations among individuals for monetary dividends, rather than mutual responsibilities to other related human beings.

Conclusion

In this chapter, I have argued that the Treaty settlements process has been used by the Crown as a conduit for neoliberal policies and practices. The Crown has transformed discussions regarding Te Tiriti breaches and tino rangatiratanga into negotiations regarding transfers of assets. The Crown has also insisted upon the adoption by tribal organisations of corporate structures which, it argues, will assist Māori to achieve development. However, this insistence does not correspond with evidence of the effects of neoliberal practices on Māori, which are predominantly negative, and deny

Māori the opportunity to continue to pursue forms of governance that are contrary to neoliberalism. Māori are treated as citizens, but only insofar as this allows them to be neoliberal citizens. Māori are treated as tribal members, but only insofar as this allows the tribe to be corporatised. While neoliberal policies recognise and pay attention to Māori structures of governance, this is not a respectful interaction, nor is it two-way, except insofar as neoliberal advocates make rhetorical concessions in order to gain support for and maintain the implementation of their policies.

To achieve recognition, visibility, credibility and therefore inclusion within a neoliberal vista and regime, Māori are pressured to accept neoliberal values and policies. But neoliberal commodifying ideals, applied to Māori through the Treaty settlements process, have serious repercussions for Māori organising techniques and the structure of the tribe. Despite this, Māori resistance is always present in the process – upholding the kinds of values and realities that the neoliberal framework underestimates or ignores.

Notes

1   A. Choudry, 'APEC, Free Trade, and 'Economic Sovereignty'', November 1996, http://aotearoa. wellington.net.nz/int/chondry1.html (accessed 9/1/2007).

2   Aotearoa is the Māori word for New Zealand. I use the term Aotearoa New Zealand to indicate the significance of the two nations, Pakeha and Māori. Pakeha is the Māori word for New Zealanders of European decent.

3   The Crown refers to the Executive branch of government, commonly understood in New Zealand as the Cabinet.

4   Given the *contra proferentum* rule in international law, which indicates that in times of disputes regarding versions of treaties, a decision is made against the party that drafted the document and the indigenous text takes preference. Therefore I refer to the Māori version.

5   Te Puni Kokiri, *Maori in the New Zealand Economy*, Wellington: Te Puni Kokiri, 1999, p. 10.

6   I shall specifically refer to Te Tiriti when indicating the particular points made in that specific version.

7   See the Appendix for the text of Te Tiriti. In commenting on his translation of the Māori text, Hugh Kawharu argues that, 'There could be no possibility of the Māori signatories having any understanding of government in the sense of 'sovereignty'.' Kawharu translates *tino rangatiratanga* as 'unqualified exercise of their chieftainship'. See I. H. Kawharu (ed.), *Waitangi: Maori and Pakeha Perspectives of the Treaty of Waitangi*, Auckland: Oxford University Press, 1989, p. 319.

8   Made by a number of mainly northern tribes (the 'United Tribes of New Zealand').

9   See, for example, M. Durie, 'Tino Rangatiratanga', in M. Belgrave, M. Kawharu and D. Williams (eds), *Waitangi Revisited*, Melbourne: Oxford University Press, 2005; and L. Comer, 'Te Puni Kokiri', *Kokiri Paetae*, August 2002, p. 3.

10 P. McHugh, 'Crown-Tribe Relations: Contractualism and Coexistence in an Intercultural Context', in G. Davis, B. Sullivan and A. Yeatman, *The New Contractualism*, Brisbane: Centre for Australian Public Sector Management, 1997, p. 203.

11 Ibid, p. 202.

12 P. McHugh, 'From Sovereignty Talk to Settlement Time', in P. Havemann (ed.), *Indigenous Peoples' Rights in Australia, Canada and New Zealand*, Auckland: Oxford University Press, 1999, p. 460.

13 Copies of the Deeds of Settlement can be found at the office of Treaty Settlements website, http://www.ots.govt.nz/frameset-settlementdocs.html (accessed 6/9/2006).

14 W. H. Oliver, *Claims to the Waitangi Tribunal*, Wellington: Waitangi Tribunal Division, Department of Justice, 1991, p. 10.

15 Ibid.

16 See D. V. Williams, *Te Kooti Tango Whenua: The Native Land Court 1864-1909*, Wellington: Huia Publishers, 1999.

17 P. Joseph, 'Māori and the Market: the Waitangi Tribunal', *Race and Class*, Vol. 41, No. 4, April-June 2000, p. 61.

18 L. Watson, 'The Negotiation of Treaty of Waitangi Claims: An Issue Ignored', *Otago Law Review*, Vol. 8, No. 4, 1996, p. 618.

19 Waitangi Tribunal, *Muriwhenua Report, 1988*. Available at the Waitangi Tribunal website, http://www.waitangi-tribunal.govt.nz/ (accessed 21/12/2005).

20 Oliver, 1991, p. 34.

21 J. McGuire, 'A Theory For a More Coherent Approach to Eliciting the Meaning of the Principles of the Treaty of Waitangi', *NZLJ*, 1996, 116.

22 P. Harris and S. Levine (eds), *The New Zealand Politics Source Book*, 2nd ed., Palmerston North: Dunmore Press, 1994, p. 354.

23 The Crown had protected land claims lodged prior to 1986 but did not secure those after. *New Zealand Maori Council v Attorney-General* [1987] 1 NZLR 641-719.

24 Ibid, pp. 663-664.

25 *Wi Parata v Bishop of Wellington* [1877] NZJR (NS) 78.

26 J. Kelsey, *A Question of Honour? Labour and the Treaty 1984-1989*, Wellington: Allen and Unwin, 1990, p. 85.

27 'Hirangi 1996', Unpublished notes prepared by the convenors' group, p. 8.

28 A. Ward, *An Unsettled History: Treaty Claims in New Zealand Today*, Wellington: Bridget Williams Books, 1999, p. 30.

29 M. E. Lashley, 'Implementing Treaty Settlements via Indigenous Institutions: Social Justice and Detribalization in New Zealand', *The Contemporary Pacific*, Vol. 12, No. 1, 2000, p. 32.

30 See, for example, R. Douglas, *Unfinished Business*, Auckland: Random House, 1993, pp. 208-214.

31 Office of Treaty Settlements, *Crown Proposals for the Settlement of Treaty of Waitangi Claims*, Wellington: Crown Copyright, 1994.

32 Ibid.

33 M. Durie, *Te Mana, Te Kawanatanga: The Politics of Maori Self-Determination*, Auckland: Oxford University Press, 1998, pp. 190-194.

34 Ward, 1999, p. 52. Paul Joseph places the figure at closer to $66 billion. Joseph, 2000, p. 72.

35 Waitangi Tribunal, *Report of the Waitangi Tribunal on the Manukau Claim*, 2nd ed., Wellington: Waitangi Tribunal, 1989, p. 87.

36 Hirangi, 1996. Also see R. Walker, 'Māori Sovereignty, Colonial and Post-Colonial Discourses', in Havemann, 1999.

37 Durie, 1998, p. 235.

38 Treasury, quoted in Kelsey, 1990, p. 251.

39 See for example, M. Jackson, 'Smashing Cups and Muriwhenua', *Kia Hiwa Ra*, May 1997, p. 25.

40 M. Jackson, 'Māori Can and Will Say "No"', *Kia Hiwa Ra*, September 1997, p. 17.

41 M. Jackson in G. McLay (ed.), *Treaty Settlements: The Unfinished Business*, Wellington: New Zealand Institute of Advanced Legal Studies, p. 157.

42 Law Commission, *Maori Custom and Values in New Zealand Law*, NZLC SP9, Wellington: Law Commission, March 2001, p. 95.

43 A similar point was made in the Canadian *R v Sparrow* judgment, which stated that 'it is possible, and indeed crucial, to be sensitive to the aboriginal perspective itself on the meaning of the rights at stake'. *R v Sparrow [1990] 1 SCR 1075.*

44 I. Macduff, 'The Role of Negotiation: Negotiated Justice?', in McLay (ed.), 1995, p. 54.

45 T. Dare quoted in D. Barber, 'Māori: The Corporate Warrior', *Management*, February 1993, p. 40.

46 D. Awatere-Huata quoted in H. Melbourne, *Maori Sovereignty: The Maori Perspective,* Auckland: Hodder Moa Beckett, 1995, p. 181.

47 T. Henare quoted in *Kia Mohio*, No. 2, July 1997, p. 1.

48 R. C. A. Maaka, 'The New Tribe: Conflicts and Continuities in the Social Organisation of Urban Māori', *The Contemporary Pacific*, Vol. 6, No. 2, Fall 1994, p. 316.

49 See, for examples, the Hui Taumata website, www.huitaumata.maori.nz (accessed 18/9/2006).

50 See, for example, T. O'Regan, 'The Evolution of the Tribe: The Challenge for an Old Culture in a New Century', Freilich Foundation lecture, Canberra, 31 May 2001; R. Maaka and A. Fleras, 'Politicising Property Rights: Tino Rangatiratanga as Post-Colonizing Engagement', *Sites*, No. 35, Spring, 1997.

51 Some scholars argue however that given Te Tiriti was between the Crown and hapū rather than iwi, hapū should be the entity central to negotiations. See, for example, Watson, 1996, p. 618.

52 McHugh, 1997, pp. 205-206.

53 For a discussion of tribal committees and their interaction with the Crown and attempts to regulate in the 19th century, see V. O'Malley, *Agents of Autonomy,* Wellington: Huia Publishers, 1998.

54 K. Gover and N. Baird, 'Identifying the Māori Treaty Partner', *University of Toronto Law Journal*, Vol. 52, 2002, p. 51.

55 Maaka, 1994, p. 324.

56 See, for example, T. Hazledine, *Taking New Zealand Seriously: The Economics of Decency*, Auckland: Harper Collins, 1998.

57 Office of Treaty Settlements, 1994, p. 13.

58 Ibid, pp. 45-46.

59 Māori Economic Development Commission, 1999, p. 12.

60 Translated as 'a place to stand'.

61 O'Regan, 2001.

62 Ibid, p. 16.

63 E. T. Durie, 'Will the Settlers Settle? Cultural Conciliation and Law', *Otago Law Journal*, Vol. 8, No. 3, 1995, p. 454.

64 Ibid, p. 455.

65 Marae are tribal meeting houses/places.

2

Economic Determinants of Māori Health and Disparities[1]

Bridget Robson

Introduction

An overview of health trends shows that since the mid-1980s, the point at which neoliberal policies began to be implemented in earnest, disparities between Māori and non-Māori in terms of health have increased significantly, as measured by the key indicators of life expectancy, cancer mortality and cardiovascular morbidity and mortality. Research also shows a disturbing trend in the provision of health services, whereby higher levels of Māori ill-health do not correspond with higher rates of access to health services.

This chapter examines such disparities not in order to compare Māori with non-Māori, but rather to analyse how resources that impact on health become distributed unevenly between the Māori and non-Māori populations. The approach assumes that ethnic health inequalities are the result of the unequal distribution of the economic, social, environmental and political determinants of health (including access to effective, high-quality health and disability services).[2] It seeks to further our understanding of the forces driving the differential distribution of economic determinants of health in particular.

While a causal link may not be able to be conclusively drawn between neoliberal policies and worsening trends in Māori health, this chapter encourages serious consideration of those trends which neoliberal policies may be exacerbating. In addition, it suggests a closer examination of the kinds of inequalities that may underpin the health system, which, in turn, support neoliberal practices.

Māori development is set in a context of inequality in Aotearoa New Zealand.[3] The political economy is based on the colonisation of Māori. Such structures mean that many Māori are already more vulnerable than Pākehā to the effects of neoliberalism.[4] As a result, Māori 'choices' are restricted from the outset. The most obvious example is in the labour market. Māori have low formal educational qualification rates compared with Pākehā, and are clustered in industries where labour is often temporary, insecure, low paid and expendable.[5] The neoliberal restructuring process resulted, both directly and indirectly, in the loss of thousands of jobs.[6] In particular, those industries where Māori workers were concentrated, such as the manufacturing sector and state industries such as railways, forestry, and public works, were forced to lay off staff.

The consequences continue to perpetuate the inequalities experienced by Māori. High levels of unemployment and of consequent reliance on assistance from the state make them targets for criticism from neoliberal advocates, and vulnerable to reductions and restrictions in welfare spending.[7] The impact of the high social costs arising from this situation can be seen in housing, education, and health statistics.[8]

In a 2003 paper, King reviewed evidence of the associations between economic determinants and health outcomes in New Zealand and internationally, possible explanations for these associations, and evidence for the effects of government social and economic policy on health outcomes.[9] King found clear associations between health outcomes and economic determinants such as income, education, employment, occupation, housing conditions and locality of residence. These factors have greater explanatory power in combination than in isolation, and have a cumulative effect over the life course. However, ethnicity has an independent effect over and above that explained by the other factors. Countries that have pursued redistributive policies generally have lower rates of poverty and better health outcomes. No evidence was found that social spending inhibits economic growth. King concluded that increased unemployment, casualisation of work, reduced wages, reduced benefits, tightened benefit targeting with multiple abatement regimes, and higher accommodation costs exacerbated levels of poverty and inequality in New Zealand during the 1980s and 1990s, and very likely adversely affected population health.

The story of economic determinants and health is also the story of Treaty rights and breaches, human rights, indigenous peoples' rights and ethical obligations. Recent struggles concerning title to the seabed and foreshore, and the commercial and political interests being served, provide a stark reminder that colonialism has been a continuous force impacting on Māori economy and health since the early nineteenth century, echoing the histories of indigenous nations in settler colonial lands throughout the world.

This chapter draws on international and local literature relating to indigenous peoples and ethnic disparities in health. Indigenous values and concepts relating to the economy and to health do not necessarily equate to the values underpinning the published literature on economic determinants of health. The tensions inherent in this disjunction are recognised by highlighting the voices of indigenous commentators throughout the chapter.

The land itself was, and is, the source of life: Papa-tū-ā-nuku is the Earth Mother from whom we all come and to whom we all return. The placenta that nurtures us before birth and the land that provides nourishment in life are both whenua. The whenua provides its gifts, or taonga, to us as koha – as something which must be reciprocated. The exchange is an obligation on humans to care for the earth so that its resources will continue to be available. With this obligation goes a realisation that the iwi and the whenua are interdependent and exist in harmony only as long as their relationship is in balance. Thus Māori are tangata whenua. Not people *in* the land or *over* the land, but people *of* it.

Moana Jackson[10]

Many indigenous nations are struggling with the realities underpinning the statistics reflected in this chapter. These nations' histories resound with stories of resistance, consistent and ongoing reaffirmation and assertion of rights and renewal of relationships with the environment, tupuna and the generations to come.

Health trends

The impact of colonial settlement on Māori health is well established. Disease, conflict and dispossession led to a decline in the total Māori population of one third or more during the late nineteenth century. The twentieth century witnessed a regeneration of the Māori population. During the three decades after World War Two, there was a rapid narrowing of the life expectancy gap between Māori and non-Māori.[11]

Since the mid-1980s, however, there has been new and significant widening of this gap.[12] While non-Māori life expectancy at birth increased at its fastest rate since World War Two, the increase for Māori was minimal. Similarly, mortality rates declined for non-Māori across all age groups, while remaining relatively static for Māori. Thus, mortality gaps widened in both sexes and in each age group. The largest disparities are evident in the 45–64 year age groups, among which Māori rates of all-cause mortality are three times those of the non-Māori/non-Pacific population from 1996 to 1999 (Figure 1.1).

Figure 1.1: Māori/non-Māori non-Pacific mortality rate ratios 1980-1999[13]

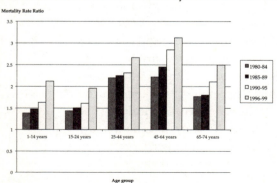

Cardiovascular disease, cancer, respiratory disease and injury were the major causes of death for both Māori and non-Māori. Cancer mortality decreased steadily among non-Māori/non-Pacific, but actually increased for Māori (Figure 1.2). The Māori to non-Māori ratio for cancer registration is lower than the same ratio for cancer mortality.[14] This pattern is consistent across all major cancer sites, and indicates higher case fatality rates among Māori than among Pacific or non-Māori. In other words, among those who get cancer, Māori are more likely than Pacific or non-Māori to die of it.

Figure 1.2: Cancer mortality, age – sex standardised rates per 100,000, ages 1-74 years, 1980-1999[15]

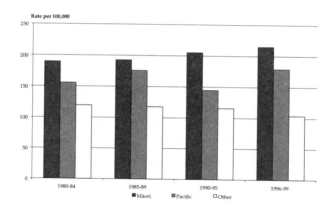

Cardiovascular mortality decreased for both Māori and non-Māori, but did so to a lesser extent for Māori. Between 1996 and 1999, Māori males' rate of death from cardiovascular disease was 3.0 times the rate for non-Māori/non-Pacific males. The rate for Māori females was 4.2 times the non-Māori/non-Pacific rate (Figure 1.3).

Figure 1.3: Cardiovascular mortality, age – sex standardised rates per 100,000, ages 1-74 years, 1980-1999[16]

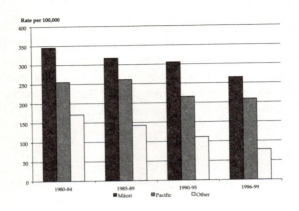

Of the cardiovascular deaths, mortality rates for stroke decreased for both Māori and non-Māori; but between 1996 and 1999, Māori males had twice the mortality rate for non-Māori males, and Māori females had three times the rate for non-Māori females. Gaps widened, too, for deaths from ischaemic heart disease: while the non-Māori rate fell substantially over these 20 years, the decline for Māori was lower, especially among Māori males. Despite the higher mortality from heart disease among Māori and Pacific, cardiac interventions were most frequently received by non-Māori/non-Pacific people during this period.[17] Figure 1.4 shows male mortality rates between 1996 and 1999, compared with publicly funded cardiac interventions for the years 1990–99. Westbrooke et al. found that these patterns of ethnic disparity held even when gender, age and deprivation were controlled for.[18]

Figure 1.4: Ischaemic heart disease mortality 1996-99 and rates of publicly funded coronary artery bypass and graft and angioplasty 1990-1999. Age – sex standarised rates per 100,000 for Māori, Pacific and other males[19]

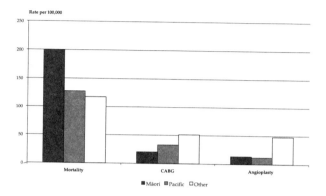

Deaths from unintentional injury decreased among both Māori and non-Māori between 1980 and 1999. However, the rate for Māori remained twice as high as that for non-Māori/non-Pacific (Figure 1.5). Road traffic crashes were the main cause of death from unintentional injury.[20]

Figure 1.5: Unintentional injury mortality 1980-99. Age – sex standardised rates per 100,000[21]

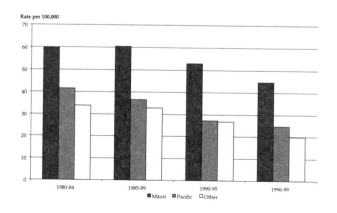

In 1980, suicide rates among young adults (15–24 years) were lower among Māori than among non-Māori. However, Māori rates of youth suicide (especially among males) accelerated from around 1985, to the point where Māori rates (among both males and females) were twice those of non-Māori rates by 1996–99. Figure 1.6 shows suicide rates for males aged 15–24 years. Similar increases occurred among Māori aged 25–44 years, although the rates are lower in that age group. Female rates are about a third as high as the male rates.[22] Male youth suicide rates may be starting to decline, but they remain higher among Māori than among non-Māori.[23] Among young women, the rate of hospital admissions for intentional self-harm is about a fifth lower among Māori than among non-Māori. Among young men, however, the rate for Māori is about a fifth higher than for non-Māori.[24]

Figure 1.6: Suicide rates per 100,000 among males aged 15-24 years, 1980-1999[25]

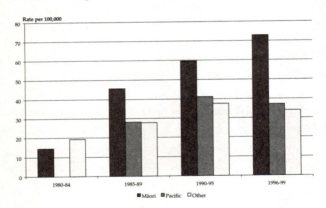

Trends in infant deaths are similar to those of other age groups. Infant deaths have decreased among both Māori and non-Māori over the last 20 years. However, because the decrease was much greater among non-Māori than Māori infants, disparities have widened considerably during this period. In 1999, infant deaths were twice as common among Māori babies (9.2 per 1,000 live births) as among non-Māori babies (4.6 per 1,000 live births).

Sudden Infant Death Syndrome (SIDS) is the main contributor to this trend of increasing disparity, as the SIDS prevention campaign has been more effective for non-Māori than for Māori.[26]

In summary, during the last two decades, rates of mortality have decreased steadily among non-Māori, but only minimally among Māori. Cancer mortality is actually increasing for Māori, while decreasing for Pākehā. Heart disease mortality has declined rapidly among Pākehā, but only slowly among Māori. Unintentional injury deaths are declining for both groups, but the gap is not closing. Youth suicide rates increased among both Māori and non-Māori, but did so at a much faster rate among Māori. The difference in life expectancy for Māori and non-Māori has grown to a gap of 10 years. Evidence that disparities are increasing underscores the imperative for action to eliminate ethnic inequalities in health.

Māori health and disparities

Tackling health inequalities between Māori and non-Māori means understanding their root causes and their effects. This section outlines several models and theories aimed at improving understandings of health disparities: Reid's model of distribution and outcome gaps; Williams' model of basic and surface causes; and theories on the impact of colonialism.

Inequalities between Māori and non-Māori health and their underlying causes provide a critical site for examination. Observations of health status or health gain for the total New Zealand population primarily reflect the status of the numerically dominant Pākehā population, and can thus obscure important information on trends in Māori health.[27] Policies that are beneficial for Pākehā health cannot necessarily be assumed to be of equal benefit for Māori health. Recent improvements in the life expectancy of 'New Zealanders' have not equally benefited Māori and non-Māori, and thus signal a failure of policy and Treaty obligations.[28]

Two types of disparity between Māori and non-Māori are evident – distribution gaps and outcome gaps.[29] The distribution gap refers to the unequal distribution of economic or socio-economic resources or circumstances between ethnic groups. The outcome gap refers to differential outcomes for Māori and non-Māori within each socio-economic category (e.g. area deprivation decile or occupational class). Outcomes might be health status, health service utilisation, or intermediary outcomes such as wages. As long as there is a gradient in health status associated with economic or socio-economic status, both types of gap need to be eliminated in order to achieve equity in health between Māori and non-Māori. If the distribution gap only is addressed, there may still be an outcome gap. If the outcome gap only is addressed, ethnic health disparities will still be present, due to the unequal distribution of the two populations by socio-economic status.[30]

The economic theory of scarcity and choice recognises that all choices involve trade-offs. Every possible alternative will involve sacrifices as well as benefits.[32] In a country such as Aotearoa, where the numerically dominant group also has dominance in political and economic power, it is particularly important to pay attention to whose interests are being served by such choices. Furthermore, the Treaty of Waitangi demands that we do so.

Tackling health inequalities requires an understanding of the underlying forces that produce socio-economic disparities. It is important to realise the

---

It was not a life circumscribed by a clock, fence, or road. But there was a law just the same. Natural Law, Creator's law.

There is no way to set a price on this way of life. That simple truth more than anything else encapsulates the Anishinaabeg people's struggle with the federal government, the miners, and the logging companies. For the past hundred years, Native people have been saying that their way of life, their land, their trees, and their very future, cannot be quantified and are not for sale. And for that same amount of time, government and industry accountants have been picking away, trying to come up with a formula to compensate Indians for the theft of their lands and livelihoods. So long as both remain steadfast, there appears to be little hope for a meeting of the minds in the next generation.

Winona LaDuke[31]

---

distinction between determinants of inequality, and determinants of health. It is only by tackling the causes of socio-economic inequity itself that socially determined health inequalities can be successfully eliminated.

Williams conceptualises the determinants of inequality as being of two kinds: basic causes and surface causes.[33] Basic causes are the fundamental factors responsible for generating a particular outcome. Changes in these forces create change in the outcome. Surface causes are also related to the outcome, but changes in these factors do not produce corresponding changes in the outcome where the basic causes remain:

> As long as the basic causal forces are in operation, the alteration of surface causes will give rise to new intervening mechanisms to maintain the same outcome ... Societal inequality will give rise to new intervening mechanisms to maintain racial and [socio-economic] inequalities in health status, even if intervening risk factors are modified.[34]

Williams' model for understanding ethnic disparities in health is structured as follows: Basic Causes→Social Status→ Surface Causes→Biological Processes→Health Status.[35] The model contends that the basic causes of differences in health are culture, biology, racism, economic structures, and political and legal factors. It requires an understanding of the ways in which social disadvantage or privilege was produced historically, and may currently be reproduced. Racism is seen as a fundamental force that shapes and reshapes other social structures, in both its institutional and individual dimensions, but the institutional is implicated as the more consequential. Surface causes include health practices, stress, psychosocial resources and medical care.[36]

This view is supported by evidence that ethnic disparities in health are sensitive to changes in ethnic disparities in economic circumstances. The mortality gap between African-American and White American men and women narrowed during the 1960s and early 1970s, in line with the civil rights movement and a narrowing income gap. In the mid-1970s and early 1980s, the narrowing of the income gap stalled, and access to social security and health care declined. Inequalities in health status worsened between the 1980s and 1991.[37] Parallel trends in terms of inequalities between Māori and non-Māori are well documented in Aotearoa.

The interlocking nature of axes of inequality must be acknowledged at this point, as well as the context-specific nature of the basic social forces that undergird collective health outcomes. Solomos and Back argue that:

> racism cannot be reduced to economic or class relations but neither can it be seen as completely autonomous from wider social relations such as gender and sexuality. This is why there is need for a more rigorous analysis of the interactions between racism and social, economic, political and cultural relations.[39]

Colonisation is a dominant determining factor in the health of both Pākehā and Māori, and is recognised as such in the literature on health and inequalities.[40] The colonisation process relies on a dehumanisation of the people of the land in order to justify the taking of resources, and is thus supported by racist ideology.[41]

Racism alone cannot adequately account for the effects of colonisation. The dispossession of lands, forests, fisheries, foreshore and seabed adds

It is said that the health of Us Mob depends on the health of our land, that if the land suffers, so do we … It is not only the degradation of the land which affects the health of Us Mob, but also the politics of the country, the control exercised over Indigenous people and the fostering of programs in which they have little say, especially at the grassroots level. It is the lack of power, the feeling of powerlessness, the overall direction of Indigenous affairs in Australia which also affect the health of the people. It is the constant struggle and battle to keep a place on the land and to feel that our place is secure that causes ill-health. It is the all-pervasive racism that strikes us almost each and every day, unless we can retreat to a homeland.

Mudrooroo[38]

up to a systematic exclusion from maintaining or developing an economic base. Land was the basis of the Māori economy at the signing of the Treaty of Waitangi, which was extremely successful from the 1830s through to the 1850s.[42] However, from the 1850s to the 1970s, confiscation of land, purchase of land at unrealistically low prices, lease at unrealistically low rents and forced individualisation of title resulted in loss of iwi and hapū control over land sales, and extensive alienation of Māori land, to the point where only 5.6 percent is now collectively owned by Māori.[43] Although compensation for Treaty breaches has been sought by iwi, settlements to date are estimated to be worth less than 1 percent of their true value.[44] Today, levels of ownership of homes, property and income-producing assets are all lower among Māori than among non-Māori.[45]

The dispossession of language, culture, democratic processes and law mean that colonisation has specificity to it – a local specificity that operates in different dimensions from the racisms against 'minority' ethnic or immigrant groups. In Aotearoa, the legacy of colonisation is one of changed environments, plundered forests, wetlands destroyed, waterways irrevocably altered, lands reshaped into the colonial landscape and a relationship with the state that has frequently been characterised by force rather than by negotiation.[46]

Economic disparities in health must, therefore, be considered in view of historical and contemporary formations of colonialism, as well as the new formations manifest in the forces of globalisation. The search for points of leverage must range throughout the surface causes, to the basic causes, including racism, economic and legal structures, through to the even more fundamental root of colonisation and imperialism.[47]

Kia tupu whakaritorito te tupu o te harakeke

There is a strong driving force among Māori for economic, educational, social, cultural and health development. 'By Māori for Māori' providers in education, health and social services are growing in number and size. Many are providing services for all

New Zealanders. Māori owned and operated businesses are increasing, and demand for education is flourishing as Māori-controlled education institutions provide effective learning environments for all age groups. Whānau, hapū, iwi and other Māori collectives are building strategies for positive long-term development.

However, Māori-led services still receive only a tiny fraction of the funding available, limiting the access of many Māori to such services, and perpetuating structural inequalities by forcing Māori initiatives to operate on inadequate funding. At the same time, educational, occupational and wage discrimination act as powerful restraining forces, restricting not only Māori access to health and social benefits available to non-Māori, but also limiting Māori from maximising the opportunities provided by Māori initiatives.

Inequalities in health are embedded in our system despite the guarantees of the Treaty of Waitangi.

Force-field theory points to the role of driving forces (forces for change) and restraining forces (forces for maintaining the status quo) in reducing inequalities.[49] When driving and restraining forces are equal, the status quo is maintained. If change in a social situation is to be achieved, driving forces must be increased or restraining forces decreased.

My generation in India, born before Independence, realises only too well that many of the functionaries of the civilizing mission of imperialism were well meaning. The point here is not personal accusations. And in fact what these functionaries gave was often what I call an enabling violation – a rape that produces a healthy child, whose existence cannot be advanced as a justification for the rape. Imperialism cannot be justified by the fact that India has railways and I speak English well.

Gayatri Chakravorty Spivak[48]

The interdependence of the education system, the labour market and the welfare state means that New Zealand's tax and transfer policies, and the way they are implemented, require careful evaluation of their effect on Māori economic status, and the flow-on health impacts. Significant widening of gaps between Māori and non-Māori in education, employment, income and housing since economic restructuring signal a failure of the welfare state.

The Crown must act to address discriminatory policy and practice across all arenas, if the right to good health for all is to be achieved. The vigour of Māori development must be supported by intensified efforts to dismantle the structural barriers identified in this chapter.

Tungia te ururua kia tupu whakaritorito te tupu o te harakeke.[50]

Notes

1 This chapter is an edited and shortened version of the second of two background papers and was originally produced for the Public Health Advisory Committee on the economic and socioeconomic determinants of health. The background papers were commissioned to review evidence of the economic determinants of Māori health and disparities. B. Robson, 'The Economic Determinants of Māori Health and Disparities: A Review for Te Ropu Tohutohu I te Hauora Tumatanui, Public Health Advisory Committee', June, Wellington: Te Ropu Rangahau Hauora a Eru Pomare, 2004.

2 National Health Committee (NHC), *The Social, Cultural and Economic Determinants of Health in New Zealand: Action to Improve Health*, Wellington: National Advisory Committee on Health and Disability, 1998; Ministry of Health, *He Korowai Oranga: Maori Health Strategy*, Wellington: Ministry of Health, 2002b.

3 By 'Māori development' I am here referring to both the ability to exercise and the actual strengthening of cultural practices and ways of organising, as well as the improvement of the health, education and general wellbeing of Māori.

4 See, for example, M. McCarthy, 'Raising a Māori Child Under a New Right State', in P. Te Whaiti, M. McCarthy and A. Durie (eds), *Mai I Rangiatea: Maori Wellbeing and Development*, Auckland: Auckland University Press, 1997.

5 This is due often to education system performance failure and labour market discrimination.

6 Te Puni Kokiri, *Progress Towards Closing Social and Economic Gaps Between Maori and Non-Maori*, Wellington: Te Puni Kokiri, 2000b, p. 21.

7 Ibid, p. 21.

8 See Te Puni Kokiri, 2000b.

9 J. King, *Economic Determinants of Health: A report to the Public Health Advisory Committee*, Auckland: Health Outcomes International Ltd, 2003.

10 M. Jackson, 'Land Loss and the Treaty of Waitangi', in W. Ihimaera (ed.), *Te Ao Marama: Regaining Aotearoa: Maori Writers Speak Out, Volume 2: He Whakaatanga o te Ao: The Reality*, Auckland: Reed Books, 1993, pp. 71.

11 E. Pomare, V. Keefe-Ormsby, C. Ormsby, N. Pearce, P. Reid, B. Robson, N. Watene-Haydon, *Hauora: Maori standards of health. A Study of the Years 1970-1991*, Wellington: Te Ropu Rangahau Hauora a Eru Pomare, 1995; I. Pool. *Te Iwi Maori: A New Zealand Population Past, Present and Projected*, Auckland: Auckland University Press, 1991.

12 S. Ajwani, T. Blakely, B. Robson, M. Tobias, M. Bonne, *Decades of Disparity: Ethnic Mortality Trends in New Zealand 1980-1999*, Wellington: Ministry of Health and University of Otago, 2003.

13 Ajwani et al., 2003.

14 Ministry of Health, *Cancer in New Zealand: Trends and projections*, Wellington: Ministry of Health, 2002a.

15 Ajwani et al., 2003.

16 Ibid.

17 C. Tukuitonga and A. Bindman, 'Ethnic And Gender Differences In The Use Of Coronary Artery Revascularisation Procedures In New Zealand', *New Zealand Medical Journal*, No. 115, 2002, pp. 179-82.

18 I. Westbrooke, J. Baxter, J. Hogan, 'Are Māori Under-Served For Cardiac Interventions?', *New Zealand Medical Journal*, No. 114, 2000, pp. 484-7.

19 Ajwani et al., 2003 and Tukuitonga and Bindman, 2002.

20 Ajwani et al., 2003.

21 Ibid.

22 Ibid.

23 New Zealand Health Information Service (NZHIS), *Suicide Facts: Provisional 2001 Statistics (All Ages)*, Wellington: NZHIS, 2002.

24 Ibid.

25 Ajwani et al., 2003.

26 D. Tipene-Leach, S. Abel, S. Finau, J. Park, M. Lenna, 'Māori Infant Care Practices: Implications for Health Messages, Infant Care Services and SIDS Prevention in Māori Communities', *Pacific Health Dialog*, 2000, Vol. 7, pp. 29-37.

27 B. Robson, *Mana Whakamaarama: Equal Explanatory Power*, Wellington: Te Ropu Rangahau Hauora a Eru Pomare, 2002.

28 Ajwani et al., 2003.

29 P. Reid, B. Robson, C. P. Jones, 'Disparities in Health: Common Myths and Uncommon Truths', *Pacific Health Dialog*, Vol. 7, 2000, pp. 38-47; Ministry of Health, 2002a.

30 C. Jones, *Maori-Pakeha Health Disparities. Can Treaty Settlements Reverse the Impacts of Racism?*, Wellington: Ian Axford Fellowships Office, 1999.

31 W. LaDuke, *All Our Relations: Native Struggles for Land and Life*, Cambridge: South End Press, 1999, p. 116.

32 P. Dalziel, *Taxing the Poor: Key Economic Assumptions Behind the April 1991 Benefit Cuts: What Are the Alternatives?*, Canterbury: Department of Economics, Lincoln University, 1993.

33 D.R. Williams, 'Race and Health: Basic Questions, Emerging Directions', *Annals of Epidemiology*, Vol. 7, 1997, pp. 322-333.

34 Ibid, p. 327.

35 Ibid.

36 Ibid.

37 D.R. Williams, 'Racial/Ethnic Variations in Women's Health: The Social Embeddedness of Health', *American Journal of Public Health*, Vol. 92, pp. 588-597, 2002.

38 Mudrooroo, *Us Mob: History, Culture, Struggle: An Introduction to Indigenous Australia*, Sydney: Angus and Robertson, 1995, pp. 126-7.

39 J. Solomos and L. Back, *Racism and Society*, Houndmills: Macmillan Press, 1996, p. 29.

40 See, for example, I. Pool, 1991; S. Kunitz, *Disease and Social Diversity: The European Impact on the Health of Non-Europeans*, New York: Oxford University Press, 1994; Pomare et al., 1995; NHC, 1998; P. Howden-Chapman and M. Tobias (eds), *Social Inequalities in Health: New Zealand 1999*,

Wellington: Ministry of Health, 2000b; M. Durie, *Whaiora: Maori Health Development,* Auckland: Oxford University Press, 1994; Te Puni Kokiri, 2000b; Ministry of Health, 2002.

41   W. Churchill, *Indians Are Us? Culture and Genocide in Native North America,* Monroe: Common Courage Press, 1994.

42   R. Walker, *Ka Whawhai Tonu Matou: Struggle Without End,* Auckland: Penguin Books, 1990.

43   A. Horsfield and M. Evans, *Maori Women in the Economy: A Preliminary Review of the Economic Position of Maori Women in New Zealand,* Wellington: Te Ohu Whakatupu, Te Minitatanga mo nga Wahine, 1988; Te Puni Kokiri, *Maori in the New Zealand Economy,* 2nd ed., Wellington: Te Puni Kokiri, 2000a.

44   M. Mutu, Keynote Address at Matauranga Tuku Iho Tikanga Rangahau: Traditional Knowledge and Research Ethics Conference, Te Papa, Wellington, 10-12 June 2004, Auckland: Nga Pae o te Maramatanga, 2004.

45   Te Puni Kokiri, *Maori in the New Zealand Economy,* 2nd ed., Wellington: Te Puni Kokiri, 2000a.

46   G. Park, *Nga Uruora: Ecology and History in a New Zealand Landscape,* Wellington: Victoria University Press, 1995.

47   '"Imperialism" means the practice, the theory, and the attitudes of a dominating metropolitan centre ruling a distant territory; "colonialism", which is almost always a consequence of imperialism, is the implanting of settlements on distant territory.' E. W. Said, *Culture and Imperialism,* New York: Vintage, 1993, p. 9. 'Internal colonialism is a form of colonialism in which the dominant and subordinate populations are intermingled, so that there is no geographically distinct "metropolis" separate from the "colony".' M. Barrera, quoted in D. Landry and G. Maclean (eds), *The Spivak Reader: Selected Works of Gayatri Chakravorty Spivak,* New York and London: Routledge, 1996, p. 24.

48   G. Spivak, *A Critique of Postcolonial Reason: Toward a History of the Vanishing Present,* Cambridge and London: Harvard University Press, 1999, p. 371.

49   K. Lewin, *Field Theory in Social Service: Selected Theoretical Papers,* New York: Harper Brothers, 1951.

50   'Set the overgrown bush alight and the flax shoots will spring up.' H. W. Williams, *A Dictionary of the Maori Language,* Wellington: Government Printer, 1985. In other words, clear away the restraining forces to let the driving forces prevail.

Part Two

Māori who live in ways contrary to neoliberal ideas implicitly challenge neoliberal practices. For those Māori aiming to live according to tikanga Māori and maintain and protect mātauranga Māori, the exploitation and domination of Māori knowledge though neoliberal practices make this difficult to achieve. Neoliberal systems of private ownership which encourage the exploitation of Māori knowledge and iconography for profit are incompatible with Māori knowledge-management systems. Cherryl Smith and Maui Solomon's chapters provide examples of everyday acts of resistance, of challenging neoliberal practices by implicitly critiquing them, as well as describing lives that neoliberal practices cannot fully extinguish. Alice Te Punga Somerville's chapter explicitly engages with resistance through telling stories and re-centring Māori concerns wherever they may be.

3

Cultures of Collecting

Cherryl Smith

We ￼

s. *Two of my cousins are the*
r they follow the migrations
year as the stocks diminish,
to the same places that our
hfully give eels out to kuia
eels served at hui anymore;
ld any eels. It's against the

> Shaneek is not going to track and field this year.

ny writing, not because
u from Kauangaroa and
vas a person who taught
still unravelling, even as
ut her and how she used
ly, she remains an anchor
to the past, just like my grandfather and the many memories we
share of all those in their generation and before them.

My brother talked about how when he went into the bush
with my grandmother to gather plants, she was very careful and
purposeful when she was there. If you went with her and you
accidentally kicked a stone or knocked something out of place,
you were shown or told how to put it back as it was. You did
not walk through the place without being mindful. You had to

walk carefully. Each thing had its place; each thing was there for a reason, the stones, the dead wood, the leaves, everything. We never spent any time conjecturing over why something was there, but it was made clear that those were not just 'things' but had importance of their own. They had an appropriate place to be. We were to respect their place in the world.

As I understood more about rocks, soil and leaves, I saw that they did have purposes, some of which we could understand by observation. Rocks hold warmth, help drainage, release heat at night and provide contours for land. A leaf provides leaf mould as a means to feed the soil and plants. Driftwood, which covers our west coast beaches in abundance, is also important because sand erosion can be mediated by the presence of driftwood. But even if they did not have a purpose that we could perceive, stones, leaves and whatever we saw were entitled to an existence that remained undisturbed by us.

As a result, I have never been a collector. I don't pick up leaves because they are pretty; I don't pick up lots of shells and display them around the home. But if you are walking down any beach, people are picking up shells, driftwood and other items, which they put into their pockets, and sometimes you see them dragging bigger pieces to cars. It is as if the beach and forest and walking places are supermarkets that have announced there is a sale where everything is going out the door free. People's homes feature collections of shells and driftwood and so on.

The culture of collecting runs deep. It runs through the curriculum of schools that identifies leaves and plants as objects of which we study the parts. It runs through the idea that it's a good enough reason to pick leaves because we want to study them by shredding them, or we want to make a stick because we want to play. It runs through the idea of nature as a large untapped resource, a free one that requires no respect and no payment. But more than that, it is a supermarket put there for our collecting purposes.

The culture of collecting is not only personal, but extends to the large-scale removal of things from our rohe (home areas).

Named as 'resources', the gravel in rivers is considered to be 'just lying there for the taking' and is removed by the truckload. Similarly, the water under the ground is considered to be free for the taking, as are many other resources.

Collectors have always extended beyond the personal to commercial interests and also state interests. From the establishment of states, there has been the collecting of data for the naming and claiming of our identities and the naming and collecting of our histories. Collecting has been institutionalised, as we see, in art galleries, museums, archives and academia. It has been important for the basis of scientific study, for aesthetic reasons, medical reasons and historical collections.

The culture of collecting was formed many years ago and was evident in early colonisation, when such things as stuffed huia birds and miniature glass cases with ferns and mokomokai were items of interest that were collected and sent off to markets in England. In that sense, there is not much that is new about globalisation that was not already being done during colonisation.

Collectors view the world in a particular way. Before the action of collecting begins, the person has designed 'the pretty', 'the object of desire', 'the resource' in their minds; they have composed collections with missing pieces; they have devised the search and the seeking. Their external world becomes a hunt, a trigger of recognition that shapes and manifests their desires. In this world, indigenous peoples live, being the collected, the named, the classified, the commons, the public domain, the protectors of the desired, the obstacles, the remnants, the fascinating, the reviled, the disappointing, the occupiers – a myriad of projections and illusions.

Twin peaks: science and religion

Within our communities, science and religion often seem to be external to our world. But science and religion have been integral parts of our communities from the arrival of the first ships of European explorers. From the time that Captain Cook arrived, specimens and data were being collected for study. Observations were being made of us and our environments. Religion quickly followed with the arrival of missionaries to collect souls.

In some quarters, it is believed that science and religion will meet and will discover the same fundamental truths. Unfortunately, as this chapter argues, the fundamental truths are underscored by the same norms, beliefs and values. Science took the low road and religion took the high road when it came to the culture of collecting. The low road was the material world, and the high road was religion. Increasingly, as global problems increase, both science and religion are proffered as the hopes of the future, the saviours to global catastrophe.

Collecting souls is also a continuity through both colonisation and globalisation. A number of evangelical religions believe and preach that the destruction of the world is inevitable, and the deterioration of social order and a decline into chaos are natural events. Once chaos has reigned for a period, the saviour will appear and take the good souls to heaven. Unfortunately, large numbers of believers affirm this and abdicate responsibility for social change. The recent upsurge in media-driven evangelism has seen the missionary work of the collecting of souls take on a new face. Evangelism has preached messages of sin, hell and the devil alongside messages of love, compassion and selfless service.

Nowhere have the promises of a saviour been more strident than in the over-the-top promises made in the new field of biotechnology. Through this, some states and corporations have said they will feed the starving, solve world pollution, create bodies that will regenerate themselves and create perfect humans.

Wandering spirits

We have been raised with a reverence and an awe of the springs that rise up from the ground. Puna in our regions are named. Stories are told of those puna and they are respected. Recently the dining room on our marae was named after a puna. There are numerous stories about puna in our area. The cleanliness of the water is diminishing as the mass usage of superphosphate is gradually contaminating the underground water. The irony of the damage caused by superphosphate in our regions is that it was mined from the home of our Pacific cousins, and they had to be removed from their islands of Nauru.

Both colonisation and globalisation were born out of the antithesis to the idea of groundedness to a place. Colonisation is a culture born of a wandering spirit, a spirit that disconnects from their place and moves elsewhere. Colonising cultures were born out of dissatisfaction with home territories, out of oppression in homelands, and out of dreams of a better life across seas and oceans. When colonisers arrived in the faraway lands of their dreams, they worked hard, finding territories that were occupied by the native others, lands filled with wilderness and forest and teeming with untapped resources. They cleared and felled, toiling to transform landscapes into the memories of home. Bringing languages and religions, they relegated all others to a heathen's death.

Many indigenous peoples talk about the fact that being born of a place and remaining connected to a place is fundamental to health and well-being. While indigenous peoples' movement to different places could happen seasonally, there was a continuation of connection to places through generations of memory and responsibility. For Māori, states of disconnection could result in illness. There are common terms for people who are considered ill through states of disconnectedness. They are considered to be more of the 'rangi' state, and lacking in presence. Terms exist such as rangirua (confusion), wairangi (mad), haurangi (drunk) and porangi (mad). Such people were considered ill. They could be wanderers with no sense of purpose. In some cases, people who were forcibly removed from their lands did sicken and die. The death rates of Māori who were imprisoned in the South Island and on the Chatham Islands after forced removal were high, believed to be not only from the harsh conditions but also from a deep longing.

With colonisation, it was the pioneering spirit that encapsulated the dreams of advancement. With globalisation, it is the entrepreneurial spirit that encapsulates the dream of roaming the world and discovering untapped resources, of being able to achieve a sense of freedom through gathering and accumulating. Indigenous peoples record the destruction of their cultures through forced or coerced removal from lands and of their languages during colonisation. This has been seen as death by removal, a disconnection of body and spirit and the sickening and death of the people. Recovering identities from forced removal has been a long-term intergenerational battle for many.

Being curious for the sake of being curious

If my grandmother was gathering plants, it was for a reason. If someone was sick and the plants were not in her garden, then she went and got them, but did so with clear understandings of the time of day, weather, phase of the moon, the plant itself, where it grew, where you could pick it from and how much. Appropriate respect was there always. Karakia and respect were given for the taking of the plants. We all still complain about the taste of them though.

If I was with her in the garden or she was showing me something such as how to scrape flax with a mussel shell, I didn't ask questions. She wanted me to observe her and follow, and often, she would put her hands over mine and make the action that I was to follow. Asking questions was considered rude in her generation. Questions interfered with what you were doing. You had to observe, listen and then do the action.

I hear quite a few of my relations telling me the same story. They had to just observe, learn the job and get on with it. They, too, notice a marked increase in the number of questions that are asked – 'why' and 'what' questions. The assumption is that such questions are signs of curiosity and intelligence and that it is healthy to ask such questions. Silence is considered unnatural, and working in silence is considered foreign. Yet silence is important, because knowing is not translated through words, but through direct observation. Silence gives us space to observe the needs of others and opportunities to observe how things change over time.

When I was at primary school, one of the activities we were required to do was to collect leaves. We were required to pick leaves of different plants, and then we had to lay the leaves out on paper, sticky tape them on and write down the differences in colour, shape, texture and how the veins of the leaves were arranged. We had to name, identify and label quite a few objects that we collected from nature. The activity always seemed pointless to me for a number of reasons. We didn't have to remove the leaves to see them. How could we know much about the plant if we were only looking at a leaf? And why was the activity so fascinating to my classmates, except that it broke up maths and other subjects?

Whānau

Gardens were everywhere (before the war). Everybody had gardens. It was fabulous just to look around and see the growth of corn, kamokamo, watermelons, kumara, they grew everything. Everybody bottled fruit. Everything from plums and peaches. There was fruit everywhere. The kids always had heaps to eat, nobody starved but you know the old story, somebody else's always taste better than your own, so if you could nick the peaches from over the fence, they always tasted better. It was lovely. I can remember, as a child, looking over and thinking what a picture it was, to see all the big gardens. When we went back to the Wairarapa we always went back loaded with kamokamo, corn, and Dad used to make sure we took plenty home. Everybody had gardens. I was only in Kauangaroa for such a short time, but I know he [Dad] used to pick up kai and take it somewhere. He probably used to take it to people who maybe didn't have gardens. I don't know, but he was always giving food away. So, they possibly all did that to the ones that were less fortunate than themselves because they always grew heaps. More than what they could ever use. They had acres of gardens. Now that I think back I am quite sure that they used to give to others less fortunate. Things weren't easy in those days although we were never ever short of food, but I know a lot of people were.[1]

One of the most fundamental things we have always understood and prioritised is whānau. Some people have suggested that the word mokopuna, the word for grandchild, be translated as 'reflections of', implying that grandchildren are a reflection of the people from the previous generations.

Whānau have, for many years, mediated the impacts of poverty and dislocation. The ability to hold on to each other has been difficult and hard fought. We did not have the stolen-generation policies that were introduced in Australia, that tore apart families as a matter of course and buried the knowledge of their identities. While this has happened to some Māori, it was to individuals, not wholesale practice. Instead, we have had the slow, trickling dissipation of whānau to cities, schools, jail and overseas. We still largely have knowledge and a good tracking system that is able to rebuild lost knowledge of whānau and re-instil knowledge. Many of us have done tracking work for those who have had to reclaim lost identities, who have had maybe a name of a person or a place and no other knowledge of who they are.

Interwoven into our languages, practices and ways of doing things has been a deep concern with the collective well-being of others. It has been through whānau, marae, kohanga reo, kura kaupapa and other Māori places and spaces that we revive and re-instil the trust and acceptance of collectivity that is constantly eroded through the prioritising of the individual and the needs of the individual.

Both colonisation and globalisation have extolled the virtues of the individual and the idea that centring on the individual is an advanced state of being. Through individual achievement, a higher state of being can come to fruition. Through individual effort, greatness is achieved. The individual will be the bright, shining beacon of leadership, approved histories and greatness. The raising of the individual decentres the collective and retells social achievement as stories of entrepreneurs, role models, leaders, history makers and achievers.

Yet we cannot achieve anything without collectivity and a deep understanding of how to make collectivity work. That knowledge needs to be more than a collectivity that is born out of crisis. The collectivity born out of crisis retains the unequal power relations that exist within communities before the crisis happens. As Māori communities will tell you, after the floods that have devastated their communities in recent years, racism does not go away in the clean-up. Māori communities already operate on the basis of collectivity, sharing and taking care of one another, hence our ability to respond well in crisis and help those who need it, to offer not just compassion, but food, shelter, clothing and marae.

The relationship between the individual and the collective is culturally defined. In colonising, globalising cultures, the individual is writ large. For Māori, whānau have never stood alone; they are intimately connected to a whole range of relationships with both the human and the natural world, connecting to 'all our relations', as First Nations people so eloquently remind us. In our genealogies, we understand the origins of all things in a broad Creation, which we act within, rather than being masters of this universe.

Short-term solutions, long-term problems

Colonisation, like globalisation, has inscribed various behaviours and ways of perceiving that go largely unquestioned in the world, both causing environmental and cultural destruction and posing solutions to them. They ignore issues as basic as understanding the importance of silence, of listening, of leaving certain areas untouched because they have stories and rights of their own, of respecting what belongs to others and of understanding that there is a place for continuity. Indigenous peoples continue to give voice to such simple and clear messages, but they still go unheard.

As a consequence, both colonisation and globalisation propose the idea that the way to solve the world's current problems will be through more of the same – individualistic achievement, exploitation of more resources and quick-fix, techno-fix solutions such as genetic engineering, opening more borders and easier access to others' territories through the mobility of cheap labour forces, and a sticking-plaster approach to poverty and environmental degradation. What currently defines the epitome of civilisation on the timeline of development is not our ability to live on the earth as beings that are able to respect the natural world, but, apparently, our ability to devastate and destroy it.

Our marae, our hapū, continue to do what we have always done, which is to hold to our own knowledge, believing in the importance of taking care of the collective, of being kaitiaki of what has been gifted to us, and trying to piece together and hold on to the fragments that remain after 160 years of colonising. We still hold to the idea that cycles of living, dying and being whānau, our lands, mountains and rivers, are fundamentally important and that our relationships with each other, with all our relations, is the most important thing. And we are still waiting for the others to catch up.

Notes

1   Paea Smith. Kuia of Ngāti Apa and the author's mother, discussing life in Kauangaroa Pa before the Second World War.

4

A Long Wait for Justice

Maui Solomon

Introduction

The Wai 262 claim to indigenous flora and fauna and associated cultural and intellectual property rights, filed with the Waitangi Tribunal in 1991, has been described by an international expert on indigenous peoples' rights as one of the most important claims of its kind anywhere in the world.[1] In 2001, the Royal Commission on Genetic Modification recommended to the New Zealand government that, due to the national significance of the Wai 262 claim to Māori, all parties should work together to ensure it is resolved as soon as possible.[2] This recommendation was adopted by Cabinet in November 2001 together with a recommendation directing all government officials to be "proactive in pursuing cultural and intellectual rights for indigenous peoples internationally".[3]

Despite its widely recognised significance both in Aotearoa/ New Zealand and internationally, the claim has suffered many setbacks over the years, including a serious lack of funding for claimant research, and ongoing delays in its completion. Sadly, since the claim was first filed 16 years ago, there have been several mate including four of the six original claimants, the original presiding Judge, three legal counsel and a number of key claimant witnesses.[4]

However, the claim is finally nearing an end. Claimant evidence was completed in 2006 and Crown evidence completed in January 2007. Closing submissions from both claimants and

Crown counsel will be heard in May 2007. It is not known when the Tribunal report will be available but given the nature of the claim and its complexities, it will probably take at least 12–18 months for it to be released.

Background to the Wai 262 claim

The Wai 262 claim was filed in 1991 on behalf of six claimant iwi. The claim began as a vision of Māori elders, including Hemanui-a-Tawhaki (Dell) Wihongi (Te Rarawa), Saana Murray (Ngāti Kuri), Witi McMath (Ngāti Wai), John Hippolite (Ngāti Koata), Tama Poata (Te Whānau a Rua of Ngāti Porou), and Katrina Rimene (Ngāti Kahungunu). These kaumatua/kuia were becoming concerned at the apparent loss of native flora and fauna to overseas interests, and the lack of Māori involvement and participation regarding decision making concerning the granting of intellectual property rights over native flora and fauna which they regarded as taonga.

The late Professor Sir Hugh Kawharu, of Ngāti Whatua, an anthropologist, linguist, and tribal elder, had this to say to the Waitangi Tribunal hearing the Wai 262 claim in May 2002:

> In my opinion the present claim has had no equal in terms of significance to Māori since the Te Reo Māori claim in 1985. Such a statement is not made lightly …

> The Wai 262 claim takes another step forward from that auspicious claim in 1985. It focuses on that simple phrase in the second article of the Māori version of Te Tiriti o Waitangi – Te tino rangatiratanga o o ratou taonga katoa. It talks of a way of life, a world-view, a culture, an identity. Denial by the Crown partner of these matters is the cause of historical and contemporary Treaty breaches.[5]

What is the claim about?[6]

As noted by Sir Hugh Kawharu, the claim is fundamentally about te tino rangatiratanga and the promise made by the Crown in the Treaty to recognise and protect the right of

Māori to be and remain Māori. Mrs Saana Murray of Ngāti Kuri said to the Tribunal in evidence that for her, tino rangatiratanga is about ensuring "Māori control over things Māori". This concept is expressed internationally by indigenous peoples of the world as their inherent right of self-determination. The claimants have also expressed their desire and willingness to continue to share their resources in a manner consistent with their responsibilities of manaakitanga, kaitiakitanga and wairuatanga. But first the Crown must acknowledge and accept that Māori have the right to exercise their tino rangatiratanga over their taonga.

The claim is founded upon the rights guaranteed in Article 2 of the Treaty of Waitangi, which guaranteed to Māori the 'full, exclusive and undisturbed possession of their lands and estates, forests, fisheries and other properties which they may collectively or individually possess' (English version of the Treaty). In the Māori version of the Treaty, the guarantee was in relation to their tino rangatiratanga over all of their taonga.

The claim is about ensuring that appropriate recognition, protection and provision is made for the exercise of Māori rights and responsibilities in relation to their taonga. This includes indigenous flora and fauna, their special relationship with those taonga, and the knowledge and intellectual property rights that flow from that relationship. The claimants assert that these are rights that were guaranteed and protected under Article 2 of both the Māori and English versions of Te Tiriti o Waitangi/the Treaty of Waitangi.

Claims over flora and fauna

Māori have an ancient association and relationship with the flora and fauna of Aotearoa/New Zealand. In a world dominated by commercial and market forces, where everything is up for sale and the genes of plants and animals are subjected to manipulation for scientific and commercial gain, Māori are concerned that their unique relationship with their taonga is being endangered. The claimants seek recognition and protection, as tangata whenua, of their rights over and relationship with indigenous flora and fauna. For example, the right to effectively participate in decision making over access to genetic resources, and to have their values in relation to the environment respected and given equal weight alongside those of conservationists. And to be empowered to fully exercise their role as kaitiaki of their own taonga in partnership with the Crown and other parties, where appropriate.

Mātauranga Māori – Māori traditional knowledge

The Wai 262 claim seeks the protection of mātauranga Māori from inappropriate use, and its control by Māori. Included in the protection of knowledge is the knowledge system itself, and its internal mechanism for transmission, dissemination, tuition and development. The evidence presented to the Tribunal has asserted that such systems existed at the time of the Treaty, but have been seriously eroded and disrespected to the point where the systems and the knowledge itself are at risk. This has been a consistent theme as the Tribunal has travelled from hapū to hapū to hear the testimony of elders.

In more recent times, there has been a growing recognition of the importance of mātauranga Māori and its relationship and relevance to Western science. As noted by Dr. Murray Parsons:

If science is the study of the world around us using a hypothetico-deductive process (the scientific method) then this is not exclusive to Western or European-derived cultural traditions but is also found in the cultures of all indigenous peoples. All indigenous peoples have science according to their needs and cultural understandings of their surroundings, the environment. The same thought processes that allowed Polynesians to voyage between the islands of the Pacific and to settle them, also have sent people into space. The term Māori Science has been used to emphasise that Māori people too used the scientific method and that it is not the prerogative of Western countries only.[7]

Rongoā Māori – traditional knowledge of plants and medicines

The Wai 262 claim also seeks to preserve and revive the practices of rongoā Māori, traditional Māori knowledge of native plants and their healing powers, and the preparation of medicinal remedies based on those plants. Māori traditionally had an extensive knowledge of plants and their medicinal uses. The term 'rongoā Māori' refers both to the practice of traditional Māori medicine and the body of knowledge behind that practice. Tohunga or traditional healers had special knowledge of herbal plants and their uses. Many if not most of the practitioners of rongoā were elderly women. As one elderly expert on rongoā Māori explained in her evidence to the Waitangi Tribunal hearing the Wai 262 claim in 1997, 'I know the plants, and they know me.' She described her power to heal as a gift from the Creator, and said that she was just a conduit between the gods and the plants in order to aid the healing process. She never sought payment for her services, as to do so would diminish the healing powers of the remedies she provided to Māori and non-Māori alike.

Challenges to this perspective on traditional healing have continued through Crown policies from the Tohunga Suppression Act 1908 (which prohibited this form of healing) to the current Medicines Act and related Crown proposal to establish an Australian-New Zealand Therapeutic Authority that will directly impact on the practice of rongoā Māori.

Genetic engineering

The Wai 262 claimants were concerned about issues of genetic engineering prior to the lodgement of their claim in 1991 – in particular, the likely prejudicial effects that the release of genetically modified organisms (GMOs) into the environment will have on the whakapapa of humans, plants and animals, on the mauri and tapu of those organisms, and on the claimants' responsibilities as kaitiaki. The claimants believe that there needs to be a great deal more research carried out under tightly controlled conditions to determine with more accuracy the long-term and cumulative impacts that the wholesale release of GMOs will have on the natural environment.

It needs to be noted here that the Royal Commission on Genetic Modification further recommended that the legislation dealing with applications for genetically modifying living organisms (the Hazardous Substances and New Organisms Act 1996) should be amended to ensure that 'effect is to be given to the principles of the Treaty of Waitangi', because, they said, the current reference in the legislation to 'take into account' the principles was 'tokenistic' and 'half hearted'.[8] This recommendation has been ignored by the government and the legislation remains unchanged.

Misappropriation of Māori cultural property rights

This past decade has witnessed a marked growth in international interest in 'cultural heritage tourism' and the use of Māori imagery, symbols and designs to promote commercial products, in order to gain an edge over competitors by associating products with the 'trendy' and exotic indigenous brand. Tourists are attracted to the cultures of the indigenous peoples, and their artwork, music and indigenous designs are becoming highly prized commodities, and powerful marketing and branding tools.

In recent years, a growing number of international companies, including LEGO (use of Māori names on Bionicle toys), Sony (Play Station game 'Mark of Kri' using Māori names and designs), TechnoMarine (watches and models with Māori names and imagery), Microsoft (use of Māori names and imagery in a computer game called Asheron's Call), a Danish restaurant (using Māori moko to promote food), Ford Motor Company (Māori inspired moko on a hot rod pick-up truck), and Fischer Skis (Māori names on skis), have used Māori designs, names and imagery to promote their products.

Māori are not opposed to the use and development of their culture and intellectual property rights, but insist that they have control over how their taonga (including, in this context, language, designs, symbols and traditional knowledge) are used, for what purposes they are used, and by whom they are used. It is offensive to many Māori (and certainly to the Wai 262 claimants) that names such as 'tohunga' are used on plastic toys, and moko are used to promote food products, watches and hot rod trucks.

Another example of misappropriation of traditional knowledge involves a German company registering a trademark over the Māori and Polynesian name 'Moana'. Moana Maniapoto, a top New Zealand and Māori performing artist and musician, was threatened in 2002 by a German-based company with a court injunction and damages of 100,000 Deutschmarks, for daring to use her own name, Moana, on a CD of the same name, which was for sale in Europe.

These cases provide examples of the inadequacies of the current system of intellectual property rights (IPR) for adequately protecting Māori traditional knowledge in the public domain, and illustrate how Māori names can be claimed and registered by others without the knowledge or consent of the guardians or 'owners' of that knowledge.

The international context

The New Zealand government is engaged in negotiations and treaty making processes at the international level that have a direct impact on Māori Treaty rights and traditional knowledge systems, including, for example, the Agreement on Trade Related Intellectual Property Rights (TRIPS) signed in 1994. TRIPS is designed to standardise western intellectual property rights (IPR) systems around the world and enhance free trade but has ignored altogether the existence of indigenous knowledge systems which cannot be adequately protected by IPR systems. For example, IPR is based on private *economic* rights which give the holders of those rights a monopoly for a limited period of time to exploit those rights. Whereas, indigenous-based rights and knowledge systems are *values* based and are integral to the maintenance of the cultural identity of the peoples concerned. They are collective and intergenerational in nature and whilst there exists the potential to commercially exploit traditional knowledge, that is a decision for the holders of the knowledge to make taking into account what is necessary to ensure that the integrity of the culture is preserved.

The New Zealand government's stance in regard to recognising and protecting the rights of indigenous peoples in forums such as the Convention on Biological Diversity, the World Intellectual Property Organisation and Declaration on the Rights of Indigenous Peoples has become increasingly hostile in recent years. This may be attributed to the negative backlash experienced over the foreshore and seabed issue, and the increasing politicisation of racial and Treaty issues in New Zealand.

As Treaty partners with the Crown, Māori assert that they need to be fully involved and to actively participate in any international dialogue or negotiations that have the potential to impact upon their rights as guaranteed under the Treaty of Waitangi.

Need for a process and framework
One of the difficulties for both Māori and non-Māori interests is the lack of any formal process for identifying where commercial operators are to go and whom they are to speak to, in the rare occasions where efforts are made to obtain approval to use traditional material and resources. One of the practical remedies that the Wai 262 claimants seek is development of a framework and process based on tikanga Māori values but which incorporates existing and new legal and non-legal mechanisms for the identification, protection and promotion of Māori taonga such as mātauranga, relationship with flora and fauna, rongoā, carving, weaving, etc. Such a process or framework would ideally be developed in partnership between Māori, the Crown, private sector and research interests, to ensure that account is taken of the rights, responsibilities and interests of all affected parties.

Conclusion
The Wai 262 claimants have been waiting for fifteen years for a resolution to what is widely regarded as one of the most important claims to come before the Waitangi Tribunal. While they have

patiently waited, some of the elders who brought the claim have passed away. Legislation and government policy that have serious implications for the issues raised by the claim have continued to be developed and implemented. Many of these issues are now being debated in international forums, such as the Convention on Biological Diversity and the World Intellectual Property Organisation, and Declaration on the Rights of Indigenous Peoples. Unfortunately, but typically, Māori are only on the fringes of these processes and have little influence over the eventual outcomes. The Wai 262 claim seeks to redress that imbalance.

The Wai 262 claimants have always emphasised their willingness to act in an inclusive manner and have felt hurt by claims from some third parties and the Crown that they would unreasonably restrict research from being undertaken or exclude non-Māori from access to flora and fauna. Similar misleading statements were made by the Crown in the foreshore and seabed debate when Māori were wrongly accused of trying to prevent ordinary Kiwis' access to the beaches. In reality, the only legal rights to have been prejudiced were those of Māori who were denied access to the courts by legislative fiat.

Māori are already actively engaged in research and development of their resources in conjunction with both Crown and private sector interests and will continue to be so. The fact that Māori are seeking to have recognised their constitutionally guaranteed rights under the Treaty is no legitimate basis for assuming that Māori will treat others the way they have themselves been treated should those rights be eventually recognised.

Notes

1 Evidence given by the late Dr Darrell Posey to the Waitangi Tribunal considering the Wai 262 claim, Rotorua, 1998.

2 Royal Commission on Genetic Modification, *Report of the Royal Commission on Genetic Modification*, Wellington: Royal Commission on Genetic Modification, 2001, p. 291-293.

3 Minute of Cabinet Decision CAB Min (01) 34/15, 5 November 2001 (obtained under the Official Information Act 1990).

4 The claimant elders who have passed away are Witi McMath for Ngāti Wai, John Hippolite for Ngāti Koata, Tama Poata for Te Whanau a Rua (Ngāti Porou), Tame Te Maro (Ngāti Porou), and Dennis Liho for Ngāti Kahungunu; the Tribunal Presiding Officer, the late Judge Richard

Kearney. Legal counsel who have passed away are Martin Dawson, David Jenkins and Gina Rudland (Ngāti Porou) who died on 24 December 2006. Sir Hugh Kawharu who gave evidence for the claimants passed away in 2006. Takoto mai, takoto mai, takoto mai rau rangatira mā. May they rest in peace.

5   H. Kawharu, evidence to the Waitangi Tribunal in the Wai 262 hearings, May 2002.

6   Important Note: This chapter does not purport to represent all the issues or views relevant to the various claims brought by the Wai 262 claimants or their counsel. It is an edited version of a report originally written and intended as a summary only for the purpose of briefing the United Nations Special Rapporteur on the Human Rights and Fundamental Freedoms of Indigenous Peoples on the current status of the claim.

7   M. Parson quoted in D. Williams, *Matauranga Maori and Taonga: The Nature and Extent of Treaty Rights Held by Iwi and Hapu in Indigenous Flora and Fauna, Cultural Heritage and Objects, Valued Traditional Knowledge*, Wellington: Waitangi Tribunal, 2001, p. 19.

8   Report of the Royal Commission on Genetic Modification, 2001, p. 308.

5

'If I close my mouth I will die': Writing, Resisting, Centring

Alice Te Punga Somerville

Near the end of his latest collection, *Voice Carried my Family*, Robert Sullivan offers a very short poem:

the crackling page

my poetry is a fire –
if I close my mouth I will die.[1]

The poem assumes that the speaker's mouth ('my mouth') is open. Indeed, the default position is to have an open mouth; the normal activity for this speaker is to tell, to articulate, rather than to be quiet. This wording produces a very different meaning from the alternatives, 'if I *do not open* my mouth I will die' or 'if I *open* my mouth I will live', because it suggests that our mouths are always already open. As readers, we have proof of this open mouth because this is, after all, a poem uttered by the speaker.

The last line of the poem presents a number of questions: who is the 'I' – the speaker – of the poem? Why would 'I' die? What are the stakes and implications of 'my' death? What makes this a situation in which I could die? What would closing one's mouth look like? What closes our mouths? How are we complicit in closing others' mouths? What responsibility do we have for ensuring mouths are open? And, in the context of this book, what does this – any of this – have to do with Māori and neoliberal globalisation?

One crucial form of resistance to neoliberal globalisation is our continued insistence on specificity, which both asserts and represents a clear challenge to neoliberalism's insistence on the infinite substitutability of one person (or neoliberal subject) for another. We can recognise the determination of neoliberalism to disallow our claims to specificity (and thereby to insist on a kind of assimilation into a universal consuming subject) from our familiarity with the assimilative drives of the colonial project. Euphemisms such as 'global village' and 'shrinking world' both depend upon and enlarge that project by which Europe and Euroamerica sought to incorporate into themselves not just resources and people, but also epistemologies. Māori writing in English[2] engages and counters this process by articulating and indeed manifesting a *specific* 'other.'

Following Sullivan's poem, this chapter explores three dimensions of Māori writing in English. The first explores the idea that 'my poetry is a fire', and foregrounds both the existence and work of Māori texts. The second, 'if I close my mouth I will die', suggests that this insistence on our own specificity happens in (at least) two ways: explicitly, as in 'truth telling', and implicitly, as in 'self-telling', or the way in which telling our own stories is in itself a form of resistance because it unsettles, interrupts, distorts and challenges. Finally, 'my poetry, my mouth' focuses on the implications of this 'other' daring to understand itself not simply as an 'other,' but as Māori. Specifically, I focus on texts written by Māori who live outside Aotearoa, in order to explore how centring Māori opens up the possibility of reframing the 'global' in 'globalisation.'

'my poetry is a fire': writing

If poetry – indeed any genre of creative writing in English – is a 'fire', what is its fuel? What is it burning? Where? One way of accounting for Māori writing in English is to construct a chronology of published texts. The starting point varies from critic to critic: it could be with Rewiti Kohere's 1951 *The Autobiography of a Māori*,[3] or Hone Tuwhare's 1964 poetry collection *No Ordinary Sun*.[4] It could be 1954, the year J. C. Sturm's story 'The Old Coat' was included in the first edition of the journal *Numbers*, or it could be 1966, the year she was the first Māori writer to be anthologised in a collection of New Zealand fiction.[5] Others will point to Witi Ihimaera's 1972 short story collection *Pounamu Pounamu*, or the performance of Harry Dansey's play *Te Raukura* in the same year.[6] I am tempted to offer 1959-ish, after the note at the beginning of Evelyn Patuawa-Nathan's 1979 collection of poetry, *Opening Doors*:

> Twenty years ago she wrote a historical novel which the publishers, Collins of London, were interested in publishing. The manuscript for correction went astray in the mail. Evelyn 'didn't have another copy nor the staying power to stick with it'.[7]

Powhiri Rika-Heke and Chad Allen both push the date back to the earliest (1955) publications in *Te Ao Hou*, the Māori Affairs magazine. This is a useful starting point, because it centres the moment(s) of writing and dissemination, rather than waiting for the later acknowledgement (endorsement?) of Māori writing in English by 'mainstream' publishing houses.[8]

While constantly focussing on starting points and early moments is important, a limitation of this approach is that Māori literary studies can tend to be framed as a recent, tenuous and emerging phenomenon. It is surely time to think about the literature as something more established than recent, more substantial than tenuous, more nuanced than emerging.[9] Another effect of constantly discussing Māori literature in English from a particular starting point, and following its development from there, is a tendency to focus more heavily on the first years of writing, and to read the more recent publications as continued manifestations (or perhaps echoes) of those works, if they are identified at all.[10] While, of course, the present writers owe a great deal to their origins and forebears in the field, a focus on earlier texts can obscure the later works, and in particular the innovations and challenges that they represent.[11] Additionally, most of the more widely known writers whose work appeared first have continued to publish since then as well, and so even within the 'core' Māori writers,[12] more recent developments and interests can be productively emphasised. Patricia Grace, for example, will always be acknowledged for her early groundbreaking work, but need not be eternally relegated to the (albeit very important) claims, politics and modes of 'Parade' and *Potiki*.[13]

Attempts to explore the role of Māori writing in English within the project of decolonisation are necessarily complex. For example, whether Māori writing in English is inherently compromised by its very form (it is written, after all, and in the language of the coloniser) is a long-standing debate. Māori writing in English is certainly a formal mongrel, drawing on Māori and non-Māori literary traditions, and much criticism grapples with negotiating these two traditions, especially within the context of continued colonialism. In the words of the introduction to *Huia Short Stories 1997*:

> [W]hat is to the fore are the subtleties of keeping faith with our tipuna when we are heir to complex cultural displacements and substitutions, chosen or imposed. [14]

Reina Whaitiri and Robert Sullivan foreground the implications of 'new' voices on the Māori writing scene in their essay 'The Forest of Tane: Māori Literature Today', published in the issue of *Manoa* they edited:

> Altogether they create a cathedral filled with song. Not only do we hear in this place the many traditional voices of the country, but new sounds are constantly arriving from city streets, from prisons, the marketplace, and corporate boardrooms. The rhythms of these new sounds are exciting and multiform, drawing on the languages and cultures that

enrich the definitions of Māori literature. For a long time, Māori literature will be occupied with reconciling and absorbing all of them.[15]

Roma Potiki writes about the 'fusion' of forms, through which something distinctive is retained, in her discussion of Māori theatre:

> [T]hey maintain a story-telling tradition which has kept flexible to meet the needs of a modern reality. Māori playwriting and plays bring together Māori ceremony and thought with British and European theatre tradition. While this fusion has produced a number of very different plays, whatever mix they have employed all operate within a Māori framework, and have whanau relations at their core.[16]

The *Te Ao Marama* editors note a similar 'amalgam', using the terms 'postcolonial' and 'postmodern' to shift the 'mixture' away from being simply Māori and Pākehā:

> It [this volume] is Māori writing at the margin, as opposed to Māori writing at the centre. But there are transformations happening which, guided by tikanga Māori, push the work beyond post-colonial or post-modern models to a new form that is an amalgam of both centre and margin.[17]

To reframe this situation, we might ask another series of questions. How do we talk about the experience of colonisation without falling into the trap of lamenting that we're 'too colonised',[18] that it's all over, lost, gone?[19] How do we talk about our past, our ancestors, our cultural heritage and concepts, without falling into the trap of over-romanticising, creating a (newly) 'authentic'[20] 'Māoriness' that excludes much of the Māori community? So many of the discussions about Māori cultural production – from determining who is Māori/ what is Māori writing, to discussing subject matter, politics, language and form – point to the 'taniwha' that Merata Mita acknowledges in her discussion of Māori film:

Identity at any meaningful level cannot be manufactured or manipulated ... no matter what destructive processes we have gone through and are going through, eventually the taniwha stirs in all of us and we can only be who we are.[21]

This cultural 'change' does not occur in a vacuum of course; it happens within a context in which the status quo is still not safe for Māori, and so the struggle for further 'change' is, while sometimes daunting, certainly necessary.

From another angle of critique, a well-deserved suspicion of literary genres such as novels, poetry and short fiction circulates widely in critical theory, not necessarily on the basis of any innate fault so much as on the basis of their being elevated as high culture by powerful institutions. Why, for example, do we (and by 'we' I specifically mean the elite, the bourgeois) pay attention to texts that are expensive, not widely read, etc., and simultaneously ignore those genres and modes of expression employed by the masses? Why are some particular forms of cultural production (opera, ballet, theatre, novels, poetry) aligned with some sections of the community and not others? This suspicion is foundational to the field of cultural studies, particularly as it grew out of a specific context in the UK, and this line of questioning has done very important work both in critiquing the relationship between culture and power (and capital), and in foregrounding the possibility of treating 'text' as a more general term (and thereby allowing television shows, popular music, advertising and so on into the field of critical vision).

However, it is too easy for these critiques – which were, after all, first constructed in order to challenge the (pale, male and stale) canon of English literature and its venerated status within powerful elite institutions, such as schools and universities – to be co-opted and used as a way to turn attention away from the exciting, engaged and (dammit!) revolutionary texts that Māori writers continue to produce. Albert Wendt talks about the important role of 'realism' in Pacific novels[22] (of which Māori texts are, rightly in this context, considered a part):

Some of these critics now dismiss our literature as being old-fashioned because they are still in the realist tradition. They fail to realize that *we have a different purpose for our literature* – a desire to explain to ourselves what has happened to us in the colonial process, and to argue for political change. We still see the novel as a *weapon for social change*.[23]

It seems useful to emphasise that his comments pertain not only to the specific use of realism in these texts, but also to the political possibilities of the texts themselves, despite – or maybe because of – their form: 'the novel as a weapon for social change'.

'if I close my mouth I will die': resisting

Dismantling images and setting up new modes of indigenous representation, in the context of a colonial environment, is always going to be political.[24] One particular phrase that often appears when writers and critics talk about the political nature of Māori cultural production is tino rangatiratanga, the phrase explicitly drawn from the second article of the Treaty. Roma Potiki writes about Māori theatre:

> In their work Māori playwrights re-assert the mana of the tangata whenua. Māori theatre can be seen as *tino rangatiratanga in action* ... a visible claiming of the right to control and present our own image and material in the ways we deem most suitable, by using self-determined processes.[25]

In his discussion of Māori theatre eight years later, Hone Kouka reiterates this claim:

> In theatre we found a tool that was able to fluently express our ideas and our concerns, and it was all under Māori control – here was *tino rangatiratanga in action* – a medium of little cost, with the ability to communicate to many and yet keep the message pure. We had found a way.[26]

The introduction to *Huia Short Stories 1995* foregrounds this 'focus' of 'the Māori protest movement', out of which the discussion of the collection is drawn: 'That focus is *tino rangatiratanga*.'[27]

The use of the phrase tino rangatiratanga implicitly challenges the coloniser: it invokes the Treaty, it centres the Māori world, it is about sovereignty, and it unashamedly refuses to be translated from te reo Māori. At the same time, as the *Huia* introduction demonstrates, mobilising this particular phrase explicitly links the production of Māori cultural texts with a broader context of struggle.[28] Rather than sitting aside from and merely reporting on or representing Māori, these texts (and the means of their production) participate actively in the resistance/sovereignty movement. Roma Potiki notes that:

> in seeking to make Māori art of integrity, all work must have political self-awareness and the deepest emotional overlay to it. The context must be truthful.[29]

Māori cultural production has been imbued and motivated by the politics of the past forty years.[30] Ultimately then, these texts are articulations *of*, rather than *about*, the struggle.

It is instructive to note that discussion about the Treaty as a document is, for the most part, located within the discourse/production of the nation state (New Zealand). Certainly this can be a good thing; coding Māori cultural production as 'tino rangatiratanga in action' is a useful and productive challenge for the burgeoning criticism about Māori writing in English, particularly as that criticism attempts to disentangle Māori texts from their usual consideration as a subset of the national literature of New Zealand. Internationally, much of the critical theory and literary criticism that seeks to explore the 'margins' assumes the 'centres' are nation states, and much of my own research and teaching has tended to focus on expounding, exploring and expanding the relationship between Māori and 'New Zealand'. This is ongoing and vital work. Perhaps we can see a parallel between the need for continued Māori struggle against the state (look no further than the seabed and foreshore for a pertinent example!), and the situation in which literary criticism and the teaching of literature (at least outside the discipline of Comparative Literature[31]) privileges the nation state, to the extent that it necessitates a challenging of that configuration. But in the context of neoliberal globalisation, which of course relies upon but also challenges and reaches far beyond the nation state, how might we think about Māori writing in English?

By foregrounding Māori experience, stories and perspectives – perhaps a Māori 'real' – Māori writers are engaged in the explicit practice of truth telling. A consciousness about realism has been a part of the literature since the first Māori writing in English was published in *Te Ao Hou*.[32] When the journal was first printed in 1952, it was imagined that it would enable Māori to show their 'reality' (as filtered, of course, through the Department of Māori Affairs). As Allen describes it:

> [W]hat is desired and later praised is the representation of 'the everyday situation' of the Māori and the Māori 'real'.[33]

That Māori cultural production records a snapshot of reality is endorsed and advocated by various commentators, including the editors of the impressive five-volume anthology of Māori writing, from the introduction of the first volume:

> *Te Ao Marama* is a marae where our writing will stand, to reflect the times, and to show others a little of what we were like during a crucial decade ... Nobody again may have such an opportunity to say to the present, 'This is how we are' – to say to the future, 'This is how we were ...'[34]

This idea of 'showing' is repeated in the introduction to the final volume:

> A witnessing of the times in the words of Māori themselves, showing the complexity that has become our world, the commonalities of kaupapa and divergences from it.[35]

Merata Mita describes the relationship between the production and consumption of 'our' texts:

We go to the cinema to see ourselves. We read the books that reveal ourselves.[36]

Roma Potiki writes about this 'tell[ing]' in terms of theatre:

Māori drama is about Māori people being able to tell their own stories.[37]

The (unnamed) editor of *Ngā Pakiwaitara a Huia 1995*, the collection of Māori language fiction produced through the same competition as that which produced *Huia Short Stories 1995*, emphasises the multiplicity of this reality:

Mā ēnei momo tuhinga e toro haere ngā āhuatanga e pā ana ki a tātau te iwi Māori o Aotearoa nei, ngā piki, ngā heke, ngā mea ātaahua, ngā mea whakahouhou, te harikoa, te pōuri, katoa, ka whakaahuatia mai i roto i ngā kōrero.[38]

Finally, in his discussion of Māori theatre, Kouka talks about reality as truth telling:

[In *Taku Mangai* there is] an unashamed Māoriness, better explained as an uncompromising evocation of a Māori experience, to the play which forces the reader or audience member to view the play through Māori eyes.[39]

Whatever direction our writers choose *we must tell the truth* of what it means to be Māori living in Aotearoa today ....[40]

This truth-telling takes many forms, including explicit treatment of globalisation. Consider the end of Sullivan's visionary poem 'purgatory', as he imagines a reversal/redemption in specifically global terms:

> Papatuanuku earth mother with child
> Give us an instant an instant
> To turn this world on its spire-
> Tower-cottage-condo-metro'd head

> The whole global culture flipped with the touch
> Of a discreet pedal and Aotearoa
> Of flightless birds, communist waka,
> And a GDP one-fifth of the flipped other
>
> Come swinging back and locked to the top[41]

The built environment of 'this world' includes religious architecture ('spire') and a procession of Western housing styles over linear time ('tower-cottage-condo'), as well as the builtness of transportation ('metro'). The railway has been, of course, a crucial dimension of the colonial project, because it facilitates precisely the kind of mobility of resources, people and capital that are central to neoliberal exchange. The built environment of 'this world' is inextricable from 'the whole global culture', which is the kind of 'global' interconnectedness that neoliberalism suggests is exhaustive. And yet, this poem imagines its reversal: impossibly, for an organism that imagines itself to be 'total,' something else ('Papa-tū-ā-nuku', 'us', 'a discreet pedal') intervenes, and it is 'flipped' by the tool of its own specificity ('Aotearoa/ of flightless birds …'). By naming the interconnectedness of globalisation ('this world' and 'the whole global culture'), Sullivan in fact produces and reinscribes space – and people ('us') – *outside* of that mechanism.

As we think about the role of Māori writing in English, Sullivan describes this current time as set aside as 'purgatory' – an in-between time – at the same time as he draws on Māori cosmologies. Tangaroa, Tane Mahuta and Papa-tū-ā-nuku are all there. This is an example of the 'fusion' described earlier, in which Māori and non-Māori traditions are drawn together. Significantly, though, this drawing together does not produce a stalemate or hybrid, but a 'weapon' (to quote Wendt) 'for social change'.

As well as truth-telling, in which writers explicitly treat particular aspects of globalisation, the dynamic of (what I'm calling) self-telling is another crucial dimension of resistance. By writing our own stories, we implicitly counter the stories told about us. Grace and Ihimaera have both remarked – sixteen years apart – how the sheer production of Māori texts is political:[42]

> I have been accused of not being political enough or critical enough of our Pakeha-dominated society, or hitting hard enough at the very real social, economic, legal and other problems facing the Māori people today. Okay. But I say *my work is political* because it is exclusively Māori; the criticism of Pakeha society is implicit in the presentation of an exclusively Māori values system.[43]

> When you write about people who are powerless; people to whom survival is a constant struggle; people whose values are not valued by wider society; people whose status, language, self-esteem, confidence, and power have been removed from them; then *writing will always be political* in its own way.[44]

In another place, Patricia Grace talks about the potential and necessity of representing reality in order to embrace the 'whole' Māori experience:

> We write what we know, and what we know is who we are. We are our ancestors, we are our families, we are our communities, we are our kids on the street, our nephews in gangs, our achievers, our politicians, our corner stores, our supermarkets, our news on television.[45]

Significantly, Grace does not refer to an individual experience of reality; every noun and pronoun in her list is pluralised. The 'we' is equated with several aspects of the community, from 'ancestors', 'families' and 'communities' (the latter two are not temporally or spatially restricted) through people of the contemporary moment, to the known environment – both rural ('corner stores') and urban ('supermarkets') – to the stories about the Māori community ('our news on television').

The multiple dimensions of this world are included in the scope of what it is to be Māori (including the 'kids on the street' and 'nephews in gangs' as well as the 'news on television'), and this is achieved by claiming to *be* them ('we are' [46]), rather than writing *about* or even against them. Her refusal to distinguish between people and the stories ('news') told about them ('what we know is who we are') folds back on her own argument; if the stories are part of the 'what we know' about which Grace writes (this is reinforced by the pronoun in 'our news', as opposed to news about us), then her stories *about* the stories (i.e. Grace's fiction) are a part of 'what we know' as well. Thus, at the same time that 'reality' has become a part of Māori writing, the writing has become a part of the scope of Māori 'reality'.

Not only is writing in English a means by which Māori can 'truth-tell' to other Māori, but it also grants non-Māori access to Māori. This kind of access is set up and given an authenticity seal of approval when Orbell exclaims to the − implicitly white − readers of her 1970 anthology, *Contemporary Māori Writing*, that:

> ... in the attitudes that they have in common, and also in the ways in which they differ, the writers in this collection provide a convincing portrait of Māori life. [47]

The need for a portrait to be 'convincing', or even to be a 'portrait' of 'Māori life', persists. In his 1999 address to the New Zealand Library Association, Ihimaera argues that Māori writers write for both a Māori and a New Zealand audience, and emphasises the 'decolonising' effect of Māori texts for non-Māori as well as Māori:

> Māori writers have played a major role in the stories we [New Zealanders] tell about ourselves. They have also made it easier to 'see' Waari [Ihimaera's pseudonym for Māori subjectivity]. Their major corrective has been to Write the Māori Story from the Inside. To construct a Māori world that is *validated* by *authentic* Māori experience. To offer characters who are not bit players in Pakeha texts (as villain or plot device or exotic colouring or, worse, friendly sidekick) but the main characters − heroes, heroines and, yes, even villains − in texts

of their own. To offer themes of decolonisation, antidotes and antivenemes which unpoison the stories which have been told about us.[48]

The act of 'unpoison[ing]' is important because representations in Māori literature are not produced in a historical vacuum; Māori writers are writing into/against images of Māori – created by both non-Māori and Māori – that have been unhealthy/unfair/untrue. Not only is the idea for Māori to show 'how we are', to quote Grace's story 'Parade', but it is also to show how we are *not*, through the dismantling of stereotypes and the recognition of distorted images.

'my poetry ... my mouth': centring

When we get to tell our own stories, we get to do new things. In particular, once we get to talk about writing on its own (and our own) terms, we can no longer be relegated to being a subsection of New Zealand literature (in the bookshop, the anthology, the curriculum). Importantly, once 'Māori' is wrested away from being subsumed by 'New Zealand', we then get to talk about Māori writing in English that is produced outside the political boundaries of the nation state. Reframing the 'global' in globalisation, then, is one possibility of paying close attention to the body of texts we might call Māori writing in English. The opposite of globalisation isn't parochialism; indeed, it has no opposite, and is but one model for global and inter-community relationship, mobility and exchange. When we look to Māori writers outside Aotearoa, we can see an engagement with the globe that isn't the same as engagement with the particularities of globally-oriented neoliberalism. Māori have indeed travelled globally ever since first contact with Europeans (and before that, if we include our migrations through the Pacific to Aotearoa), and recognising the long-standing communities of Māori outside Aotearoa is a challenging but productive prospect. Indeed, these Māori writers who write outside the political boundaries of New Zealand challenge us to recognise the multiple ways of negotiating the global, other than that dominant system underpinned by neoliberal and capitalist mechanisms.

Turning close attention to Australia-based writer Jean Riki's short story, 'Te Wa Kainga: Home'[49] provides an opportunity to consider the implications of centring Māori to the extent that we think far beyond the limits of political boundaries and national histories. While the inclusion of the story in a volume entitled *Waiting in Space: An Anthology of Australian Writing* marks it as an explicitly Australian text, Riki's perspective on Australia is deeply inflected by specifically Māori identity. The story is divided into three sections, the first of which begins with the phrase 'The way of the story is this'. It then recounts a story drawn from Māori oral literature, which in turn figures the 'way' of the 'story' set in urban Sydney, which occupies the remainder of the text. This is an explicit enactment of the point that Māori outside Aotearoa retain Māori structural dimension, even if the subject matter is new.

The original framing story is about 'Hinenui te po, goddess of the Underworld', who dreams, while she lies in Rarohenga ('that sunless place through which only the dead will pass')[50] that she is:

> … sitting on a rock at the edge of the sea, the place ruled by Tangaroa, te moana.
>
> A cloudless sky lightens in hue, for the sun had risen, blocking her vision for a moment with the brilliance of its rays. Her uncovered shoulders submit to the warmth of its touch because, in the realm of dreaming, all things are possible.[51]

The second and third sections are both inflected by the structure of this story, and both start with a short poem. In particular, each section narrates an interaction made possible by being forced by the structure of the city to 'wait':

> You do a lot of waiting when you live in the city… Living in the city means you are always waiting, waiting, waiting. Franz Kafka believed that time spent waiting was a break from the

business of living. He believed that we should cherish these breaks because they unburden us from the toil of our everyday existence.[52]

The first section suggests the possibilities of exchange and mobility both expressed in, and exemplified by, Māori writing in English. Just as Sullivan draws on Māori and non-Māori cosmological traditions in 'purgatory', Riki draws confidently on two literary traditions: the oral literatures about Hinenui te po, and the European written literary tradition as represented by Kafka. Riki's ability to negotiate this double influence (which parallels, of course, the double influences on any colonised person both from the colonised and coloniser) suggests a careful and nuanced sense of relationships between these traditions. The texts of Kafka and about Hinenui te po, as well as the bodies of both Riki (the writer) and Marama (the character), do indeed circulate *globally*, but the specificity of Riki's account prevents the absorption of the narrative into the simple and bland meta-narrative of *globalisation*.

Although Kafka's sense of waiting, as a 'break from the business of living', gestures towards the significance of 'waiting', it cannot speak to the colonial and economic situation of diasporic Māori in urban Sydney; this section is followed by the words:

But then Kafka never had to wait for the 380 bus to Bondi at 4am in the winter cold of a Darlinghurst morning.[53]

There is no 'break from the business of living' for the indigenous person living in a colonial context; full retreat from that context is impossible. Rather than experiencing empty 'breaks', in the second and third sections of the short story, a few moments with someone who is 'accidentally' encountered when made to wait brings about a new sense of identification and connection. The encounters are fleeting, like the 'sun ... blocking [Hinenui te po's] vision for a moment with the brilliance of its rays', although the 'vision' that is 'block[ed]' is that of 'everyday existence', which in turn enables a new kind of vision. The 'business of living' is both escaped and underscored by these encounters, and the return to 'everyday existence' is with this renewed vision that is not clearer as much as it is deeper.

The second section begins with a poem entitled 'Tama's hands' and focuses on a train ride. The poem foregrounds the theme of disconnection, and introduces the connection and 'waiting' on which the section focuses:

> Brothers, sister
> Indigenous child
> on foreign shores
> cut off from your roots
> walking among the briefcases and the suits ... [54]

Briefly, Marama – whose name means light or understanding – is on her way home with bags of groceries when the train she is riding stops in a tunnel and the lights go out; the darkness of the train carriage evokes Rarohenga, 'that sunless place'. It is this forced 'waiting' that brings about the first chance encounter:

> Marama can feel a hand snaking over her shoulder in the direction of her open handbag. The lights come back on. Marama grabs the wrist of a tattooed hand ... The hand beneath the tattoos is poly-brown, like her own. The owner is a young Māori boy, decked out in Nike tracksuit and T-shirt dominated by the words, Once Were Warriors. Now and Forever.[55]

Marama questions the boy, Tama, about the meaning of his tattoos: '"Tama, do you know what these tattoos stand for?" Her voice is shaking, "Not until you tell me what these tattoos mean"'. He knows nothing about them, having acquired them from a 'mate of mine's girlfriend'.[56]

In the context of Australia, Marama and Tama are deemed generically indigenous (people on the train don't intervene in their heated encounter, 'as if adhering to an unspoken, silent agreement that forbids their involvement in a public display of aggression, especially if this display is between two black people'),[57] and yet the basis of their connection is not generally indigenous, but very specifically Māori; they are not 'black'[58] but 'poly-brown'.[59] Tama eventually struggles free of Marama's grip, and she is left on the train, imagining two specific images: Tama's acquisition of the tattoos, and the traditional tattooing of a 'young Māori warrior'.[60]

> [Marama's] tears come for the men and women, for Tama's and her own ancestors, their tupuna, who underwent great physical pain for the honour of being tattooed with their whakapapa, their genealogy.[61]

The explicit relationship between tattoos and whakapapa suggests that the interaction about the acquisition of tattoos speaks also to the dispossession that results from not knowing one's whakapapa. Finally, the 'break' achieved through being forced to wait is ended, and 'Marama weaves her way through the seats and steps from the train.'[62]

The possibilities of global engagement other than those engagements required by the movement of capital can lead us to consider more productively, and in more nuanced ways, the dynamics and possibilities of indigenous–indigenous connection.[63] The third section starts with a poem that brings together the overarching theme of 'cherish[ing] these breaks' of waiting and the title of the story:

An Hour to Kill
Home is where the heart is
home is where the heart
home is where the
home is where?
Home is
home ...[64]

Marama sits with Nick – their relationship becomes more clear as the narrative progresses – on a park bench in Hyde Park,[65] and their 'waiting' seems more in line with Kafka's 'break from the business of living':

They have an hour to kill before the cinema session begins. They take the time to absorb what is around them in their own silent way.[66]

A leisurely description of various goings–on around the park is interrupted by the approach of an old man:

An Aboriginal man with grizzled greying afro hair approaches the couple on the park bench. He's a little shaky on his feet. Behind him, the Sydney skyline looms large, like the skeletal remains of a capitalist banquet.[67]

The description of Sydney as 'skeletal remains' and an earlier description of the 'dying light of an autumn afternoon' again parallel that of Rarohenga, 'that sunless place through which only the dead will pass'. As she did with Tama, Marama comments on the man's skin as a first point of connection. In a general sense it is 'dark', but it is not 'poly-brown' like theirs: 'His skin is so dark that if skin were a drink, his would be hot chocolate'.[68] The remainder of the story is interspersed by brief ongoing descriptions of the other activities in the park, which broadens the scope of who might also be 'waiting'; this becomes one story of many possible stories of connection and disconnection in the Sydney landscape.

After Ron asks for a cigarette and they give him one, 'Nick asks the man to sit in the space left on the bench' and Ron 'wait[s]' with them; he too enjoys a 'break from the business of living'. As it is for Marama, for Ron this 'break' is an opportunity to dwell on less mundane matters ('He sits on the park bench and begins to tell Marama and Nick about his life'), and yet it is inextricable from the 'business' of colonialism ('For their sakes he does not tell them all of it'):

Ron's people have land north of Sydney. He comes to the city for a change of pace, to see his kids, to pop in on his older sister, to wipe himself out with his brown bottled pain relief. And to remember.[69]

He narrates the story about how his 'missus', Daphne, passed away. In contrast to Tama's lack of knowledge about his background, Ron's indigeneity is located in a specific place, and as he shares his story, Marama makes connections between his background and her own. First, the connection is on the basis of similar feelings of connection to their respective lands:

'Is your homeland near the sea, Ron?' asks Marama. She is thinking of her own homeland, Aotearoa, Maui's fish, te ika a Maui, that floats in the blue warmth of the Pacific Ocean.[70]

Notice that she is talking here about her 'homeland', not her 'home'. Ron's response reframes the scale of the city skyline in relation to the natural features of his homeland, and like Marama, his focus is on his 'own homeland':

The sea?' he asks. 'You wanna know about the bloody sea, you should come and see my place up north sometime. Do ya surf, Nick? Man, you should see the waves we get. Bigger than any of those bloody things!' He makes a sweeping arc with his arm across the skyscrapers that make up the Sydney skyline. It appears that concrete and steel are no match for the waves they have up north.[71]

In this moment, the text allows the possibility not only for Māori specificity (and, thereby, the gist of resistance to colonialism/neoliberalism), but also for indigenous–indigenous connection without that relationship being triangulated by the colonial powers. After acknowledging their 'own homeland[s]', the connection between Marama and Ron as indigenous people is made possible:

'Are you Maori, Marama? You are! Hey, I'm going to a hangi tonight.'

'Lucky you. I haven't been to one for ages.'[72]

Finally, the time of 'waiting' – the 'break from the business of living' – is over: 'The Town Hall clock strikes away the hour'.

Marama and Nick leave, and they leave Ron in the space where they took their 'break':

> They turn back to see Ron standing by the park bench. He is watching them leave and is waving his arm in a farewell.[73]

Marama and Nick are not unchanged by their encounter with Ron; his discussion of the sea inflects the description of their movement to the cinema:

> [Marama's] words are drowned in a sea of exhaust fumes ... Marama and Nick surf the crowds of people on George Street until they reach the entrance to the cinema.[74]

In this story, Marama's perspective on Australia is always flavoured by her being Māori; her connection with the place (through Ron in this case) is through that perspective. But Tama is also trying to keep up a connection with Aotearoa, even if his connection is through different symbols (his tattoos, the *Once Were Warriors* T-shirt). His negotiation of his own participation in globalisation is certainly framed by Marama (and perhaps by Riki) as somehow less successful than Marama's, and yet it is compelling to try to read against this as well. Despite the several ways in which one can belittle his location (he is described as a potential thief, not only of Marama's handbag, but also of the original meanings of the tattoos he wears), Tama has sought and constructed a way to claim specificity through his manipulation of these symbols, which he has gained via the commodification and global distribution of 'tribal' tattoo art and *Once Were Warriors* merchandise, both of which, in turn, trade on their novelty value as instances of the colonially imagined savage. Does Tama retain agency in this context? If we are serious about finding ways to centre Māori, perhaps the burden is on us, not him, to recognise the ways in which his claims at specificity – as specifically Māori – can potentially rupture and constrain the project of globalisation.

Centring Māori is neither limiting nor parochial: it shifts the frame of the debate, and enables us to explore more carefully the relationship between Māori and non-Māori, without necessarily routing those relationships through the metropole. When we put ourselves at the centre, as do so many Māori writers, we can reconfigure the ways in which we talk about the 'globe' in globalisation; we can operate according to different compass bearings and different tikanga.

'the crackling page'

It is easy to think that engagement with 'serious' issues such as neoliberal globalisation should be dealt with by 'serious' disciplines, in the light of which literature and literary studies might be framed as luxuries. Who has time to pay attention to the cute little poems and books when there are serious problems to deal with first? But that mindset is focussed on putting out fires, and the focussed exploration of Māori writing in English challenges us with pertinent questions. Where do these fires come from? How can we resist them? Where are the firebreaks? In 1978, Ihimaera and Grace both wrote of the need for more Māori writers, and laid out the possibilities of such growth for the issue of Māori representation:

> I look forward to the emergence of more writers who are Maori. Only then can the broad spectrum of Maori experience become available and the Maori map become fully drawn.[75]

> I ... feel confident that the numbers of Maori writers will increase considerably; that Maori values will be seen and our variousness become obvious. This will ensure also that the generalisations are offset.[76]

It is our responsibility, as readers and, perhaps, storytellers and writers, to ensure that we do all we can to support and foreground the 'Māori map' and 'variousness' that, at the end of the day, represent our claim to specificity, which is our best defence against neoliberalism.

The 'crackling page' risks disintegration, but more importantly, it must be reckoned with because anything on fire suggests danger more than it does destruction. The possibility of more things catching alight is the most important consideration, and from the point of view of this chapter, there is a distinct possibility that there are more stories sitting around like dry kindling, waiting to be told. When the page is 'crackling', it is no longer passive; the reader loses some agency and is compelled to react to the page.

The very existence of Sullivan's poem is evidence of its speaker's open mouth. As readers of the poem, we are implicated in the telling of it. As witnesses to this 'crackling page', we become witnesses, too, to the tangible evidence that the speaker of the poem (ourselves?) most certainly will not die. In the context of neoliberal globalisation, the challenge is not only to witness but to tell. The default position for our own mouths is to be open; if we close our mouths we refuse the opportunity to articulate our own specificity, and as the poem suggests, this can have dire consequences.

Notes

1   R. Sullivan, 'the crackling page', in *Voice Carried My Family,* Auckland: Auckland University Press, 2005, p. 60.
2   Crucially, 'English' is productively understood as the language in which certain texts are written, as opposed to the citizenship of those who have written them. I engage with literary studies with an expectation that it is, at the end of the day, about the stories 'we' tell about 'ourselves'. However, I need to be clear from the start that my concentration on writing in the English language is, naturally, going to be contrived to some degree, because the literatures produced from within the Māori community build on a much older and much more expansive tradition of cultural production that relies on a literacy – both of the producers and 'readers' of those forms – in Māori language, cultural metaphor, performance and signs. Therefore, the act of focussing only on texts written in English arbitrarily removes them from a particularly Māori literary whakapapa and also a sustained (oral/carved/woven/performed etc) Māori literary environment. This chapter provides a *brief* introduction to some aspects of Māori writing in English, and I need to be clear that what I present here is by no means the limit, extent or even tip of the iceberg in terms of work in the field in which other scholars and writers are (and in other projects, I myself am) already engaged. The opening up of pertinent faculty positions and courses in New Zealand universities, greater capacities of the Wananga system, and wider distribution of these texts outside New Zealand, promises that work in literary studies – both Anglophone and Māori – will only increase, and perhaps increase exponentially.
3   R. T. Kohere, *The Autobiography of a Maori,* Wellington: Reed, 1951.
4   H. Tuwhare, *No Ordinary Sun,* Auckland: Blackwood and Janet Paul, 1964.
5   Her story was included in C. K. Stead's *New Zealand Short Stories: Second Series,* London and Wellington: Oxford University Press, 1966. In 1966 Sturm actually had a manuscript of short stories ready for publication, but couldn't find a publisher. Single parenting and daily life 'took over' until they were finally published in 1983 by Spiral, the same collective that published Keri Hulme's *the bone people* when no one else would touch it: J.C. Sturm, *House of the Talking Cat: Stories,* Wellington: Spiral, 1983. Sturm was also the wife of James K. Baxter, the Pakeha poet

who was very influential in New Zealand letters, and their daughter Hilary Baxter has also published a collection of poetry: H. Baxter, *The Other Side of Dawn*, Wellington: Spiral, 1987. Sturm has gone on to publish two recent (and fabulous) collections of poetry: *Dedications* and *Postscripts*. J. C. Sturm, *Dedications*, Wellington: Steele Roberts, 1996; J. C. Sturm, *Postscripts*, Wellington: Steele Roberts, 2000.

6   *Te Raukura* was published two years later: H. Dansey, *Te Raukura: The Feathers of the Albatross*, Auckland: Longman Paul, 1974.

7   E. Patuawa-Nathan, *Opening Doors: A Collection of Poems*, Suva: Mana Publications, 1979. This note fascinates me: I have started to think of it as a spectral ancestor, paving the way for the Māori writing in English to follow. I look forward to investigating this case of the missing novel further. Of course, had the novel been published 'twenty years' before 1979, it would have had a significantly early position not only in Māori writing in English, but also in Pacific writing, Indigenous writing, and Anglophone postcolonial writing.

8   The first publication of a creative text in *Te Ao Hou* was by J. C. Sturm, in 1955. Actually the editors of *Te Ao Hou* were Pakeha, working at the Ministry of Māori Affairs. However, this 'endorsement' was a very important point on a continuum of publishing sovereignty; now, there is a Māori publishing company, Huia. Chadwick Allen and Powhiri Rika-Heke have done work around this early publication forum: C. Allen, *Blood Narrative: Indigenous Identity in American Indian and Maori Literary and Activist Texts*, Durham: Duke University Press, 2002; P. Rika-Heke, 'Margin or Center? Let Me Tell You! In the Land of My Ancestors I Am the Center: Indigenous Writing in Aotearoa', in R. Mohanram and G. Rajan (eds), *English Postcoloniality: Literatures from Around the World*, Westport, CT: Greenwood, 1996.

9   It seems to me that some Māori writers are making a claim that Māori writing predates their own; in particular, the device of the diary from long ago has been used in a few recent texts. As well as continuing the tradition of 'writing from the grave' that embedded diaries and journals can have in any context, it seems to me that this could also be read as an explicit gesture towards the kinds of texts that have been written by Māori – even if not circulated in the expected channels for literary scholars – that *predate* the usual timelines of the 1970s (or 60s or 50s or whenever). In particular, look to Ihimaera's *The Uncle's Story*, and Grace's *Tu*, which both contain 'diaries' written by Māori men fighting in overseas wars (Vietnam and WWII respectively): W. Ihimaera, *The Uncle's Story*, Auckland: Penguin, 2000; P. Grace, *Tu*, Auckland: Penguin, 2004.

10   Consider, for example, the predominant inclusion of Grace's *Potiki* over her later texts in literary studies syllabi in the US.

11   I am reminded of when my big sister lived in Japan for her final year of high school, as an exchange student. In every letter she would declare her intentions to give us a blow-by-blow account of her typical day there, and would start with describing breakfast. We must have read about twenty different descriptions of the morning fare in the Kato household that year, and I can still explain in some detail the thickness of the toast (my sister is big on diagrams) and what she would spread on it. However, she would run out of steam/ space/ time to conduct as thorough an account of her activities later in the day, and so would often be at about the point of describing her transport to school, and then would conclude with a promise to pick up where she left off in the next letter. Inevitably, we would open the next letter and find a drawing of a piece of toast and an interesting narrative about the appearance of her school uniform. Likewise, accounts that try to outline the 'growth'/ 'development' of Māori literature in English often describe in detail the first writers, and after that it's all a bit of a mush.

12   We might list Tuwhare, Ihimaera, Grace and Hulme here.

13   Of course, I am not attempting to draw a trajectory of Māori writing in English into a Western narrative of 'progress', in which newer writing is somehow better or 'improved.' Newer works do not diminish or challenge the mana or politics of earlier texts; and yet, a focus only on a certain set of texts, which were produced within a certain set of pressures and events, might obscure the depth and breadth of discourse. It also narrows the space for talking about changing emphases and themes in the subsequent works of writers; for example, the way in which Patricia Grace writes about kaumatua (elders) in her most recent novel, *Dogside Story* (Penguin, 2001), is different from

that of her earlier work. Similarly, Ihimaera's exploration of how to write about sexuality within a Māori context has changed from earlier work that did not engage with issues of sexuality – or perhaps, hinted and implied, but no more – through to *Nights in the Gardens of Spain* (1995) and again to *The Uncle's Story* (2001). Certainly Ihimaera's decision to rewrite his earlier works in order to more explicitly articulate a politics according to his later, more 'decolonised,' sensibility – a decision that has resulted in 'new versions' of *Pounamu Pounamu* (Reed, 2003) and *Whanau II* (Reed, 2004) – challenges the unidirectional linearity of progress on which this trajectory depends.

14   The introductions to the Huia anthologies deal with the issue in a different way; rather than seeking to determine how or whether a work is 'Māori', the emphasis is on the claims of the pieces themselves. This different focus parallels my frustration with the bulk of scholarship about Māori and Pacific hip hop, in which discussions about the production of hip hop as an anthropological phenomenon overshadow the possibility of listening to the actual words of the hip hop practitioners as prominent indigenous lyrical/ literary figures. It boils down, in both cases, to whether the academic exercise focuses on dancing around the texts, talking *about* them; or moves closer, sits down, pulls up a blanket, and listens to what they have to say. It seems to me that working within literary studies is a conscious decision to prioritise this second approach.

15   R. Whaitiri and R. Sullivan, 'The Forest of Tane: Māori Literature Today', *Manoa,* Vol. 9, No. 1, 1997, p. 76.

16   R. Potiki, 'Introduction', in S. Garrett (ed.), *He Reo Hou; 5 Plays by Maori Playwrights*, Wellington: Playmarket, 1991, p. 9.

17   W. Ihimaera, 'Kaupapa', *Te Ao Marama 5: Te Torino,* Auckland: Reed, 1996, p. 17.

18   M. Mita, 'Indigenous Literature in a Colonial Society', in W. Ihimaera (ed.), *Te Ao Marama 2: He Whakaatanga o te Ao,* Auckland: Reed, 1993, p. 313.

19   In my view, this is the trap into which Otto Heim falls, hook, line and sinker. Although he provides some interesting readings of Māori texts, his work seems intent on writing about the Māori community from an assumption of loss in a way that reminds me of 'deficit' theories in education.

20   Romanticisers certainly don't have the monopoly on creating forms of authentic Māoriness; some 'urban' writers could be critiqued for their assumption that all (or in the case of Alan Duff, all-but-me) Māori are poor, urban, violent, dysfunctional, unemployed, nihilistic and so on.

21   M. Mita, 'The Soul and the Image', in J. Dennis and J. Bieringa (eds), *Film in Aotearoa New Zealand,* Wellington: Victoria University Press, 1992, p. 54.

22   Interestingly, of course, Wendt's own work – and particularly texts such as *Black Rainbow* - has not been strictly 'realist'.

23   V. Hereniko, 'An Interview with Albert Wendt', *Manoa,* Vol. 5. No. 1, 1993, p. 57. Emphasis added. Similarly, Craig Womack writes: 'I won't bother much … with the scepticism of postmodernism in relation to history. It is way too premature for Native scholars to deconstruct history when we haven't yet constituted it.' C. Womack, *Red on Red: Native American Literary Separatism,* Minneapolis: Minnesota University Press, 1999, p. 3. Linda Tuhiwai Smith puts it this way: 'It is because of these issues that I ask the question, "Is history in its modernist construction important or not important for indigenous peoples?"… Our colonial experience traps us in the project of modernity. There can be no "postmodern" for us until we have settled some business of the modern.' L. T. Smith, *Decolonizing Methodologies,* London and New York: Zed Books, 1999, p. 34.

24   Notably, I think, although understandably, critics have not written about what 'inherent politicism', or representation of 'the real situation of Māori people' means for, for example, Bub Bridger's love poem 'Wild Daisies'.

25   Potiki, 1991, p. 10. Emphasis added.

26   H. Kouka, *Ta Matou Mangai: Three Plays of the 1990s,* Wellington: Victoria University Press, 1999, p. 13. Emphasis added.

27   Huia Publishers (ed.), *Huia Short Stories 1995,* Wellington: Huia, 1995b, p. 7. Emphasis added.

28   Womack puts this very clearly in *Red on Red*: 'Native literature, and Native literary studies, written by Native authors is part of sovereignty', p. 14.

29   R. Potiki, 'The Journey from Anxiety to Confidence', in W. Ihimaera (ed.), *Te Ao Marama 2: He Whakaatanga o te Ao,* Auckland: Reed, 1993, p. 318.

30   The historical accounts that appear in so many of the critical pieces attest to the extent to which the link between Māori writing (and theatre and so on) and the political context is seen as significant. In particular, many of the critical texts outline the relationship between the growth of Māori forms of literary and dramatic expression and the sovereignty movements of the 1960s, 70s, 80s and 90s. Allen's work is particularly interesting because he stretches the timeline back beyond the 1960s, with his discussion of *Te Ao Hou.*

31   The problem with Comparative Literature as a discipline for this kind of project is that while it doesn't privilege the nation, it does privilege a particular situation of language: it insists that any project includes more than one language, which has clear implications for discussions of, for example, Indigenous literatures produced in different nation states but in the same (coloniser's) language.

32   Of course, there is a difference between Māori 'real' and Pakeha 'real'; whereas a Pakeha realist text might privilege the absence of spiritual dimension (to the extent that its presence is coded 'magical realism'), for example, very few Māori texts exclude this from their depictions of the 'real'.

33   Allen, 2002, p. 52.

34   W. Ihimaera, 'Kaupapa', in *Te Ao Marama 2: Te Whakahuatanga o te Ao,* Auckland: Reed, 1993, p. 18.

35   Ihimaera, 1996, p. 16.

36   Mita, 1993, p. 312.

37   Potiki, 1993, p. 315.

38   Huia Publishers, 'He Kupu Whakataki', in *Nga Pakiwaitara a Huia 1995*, Wellington: Huia, 1995a.

39   Kouka, 1999, p. 23.

40   Kouka, 1999, p.28. Emphasis added.

41   R. Sullivan, 'purgatory', in *Voice Carried My Family,* Auckland: AUP, 2005, p. 57.

42   This 'covert', or perhaps inherent, politicism is slightly different from – although of course related to – the overt political issues tackled in the writing. I will not go deeply into the various political themes – besides (or not) explicit anticolonialism – that are a part of Māori literary texts, but they include: mana wahine (probably best defined as the Māori version of feminism); negotiation of issues pertaining to sexuality; and 'environmental' issues such as nuclear/ atomic testing, genetic engineering, etc.

43   W. Ihimaera and P. Grace, 'The Māori in Literature', in M. King (ed.), *Tihe Mauri Ora: Aspects of Maoritanga,* Auckland: Methuen, 1978, p.84. Emphasis added.

44   P. Grace, quoted in 'Patricia Grace Describes her Writing and her Māori Ancestry', *College English,* 1994, Vol. 56, No. 3, p.360. Emphasis added. McRae comments that Grace's writing is both gentle and political: J. McRae, 'Selected Stories: Review', *Landfall 179,* 1991, pp. 375–377.

45   P. Grace, 'We Write What We Know', *Te Pua,* No. 1, 2000, p. 60.

46   This is an inclusive 'we' rather than the coercive 'we' of the *Te Ao Marama* who recognise themselves/ourselves in Deirdre Nehua's story.

47   M. Orbell, *Contemporary Maori Writing,* Wellington: Reed, 1970, p. 8.

48   LIANZA Conference Proceedings, www.lianza.org.nz/conference99/ihimaera.htm (accessed 24/3/2003).

49   J. Riki, 'Te Wai Kainga: Home', in P. Abood, B. Gamba and M. Kotevski (eds), *Waiting in Space: an Anthology of Australian Writing,* Annandale NSW: Pluto Press, 1999.

50   Riki, 1999, p. 18.

51   Ibid.

52   Ibid.

53   Ibid.

54 Ibid.
55 Riki, 1999, p. 19.
56 Ibid.
57 Ibid.
58 In the context of Australia, of course, this implies Indigenous Australian.
59 'Poly' here is short for Polynesian.
60 Further exploration of this image of the 'warrior' would be compelling, especially given the 'Once Were Warriors' t-shirt worn by Tama.
61 Riki, 1999, p.20.
62 Ibid.
63 That Riki's protagonist interacts with this young ('dispossessed') Māori youth in the first section before going on to encounter an Indigenous Australian man (and, through memory, his 'missus'), interestingly parallels the section of Ihimaera's *The Whale Rider* in which Rawiri needs to connect with diasporic Māori in Sydney, before being able to connect with the Indigenous people in PNG. Before the second section, then, in which Marama encounters Ron, an Indigenous Australian man, Marama acknowledges specifically Māori disconnections and histories as metaphorised and exemplified by 'Tama's hands'.
64 Riki, 1999, p. 21.
65 Clearly, the English colonial history is written all over the landscape in Australia, as it is in New Zealand.
66 Riki, 1999, p. 21.
67 Ibid.
68 Ibid.
69 Riki, 1999, p. 22.
70 Ibid.
71 Ibid.
72 Ibid.
73 Riki, 1999, p. 24.
74 Ibid.
75 Ihimaera and Grace, 1978, p. 85.
76 Ihimaera and Grace, 1978, p. 83.

Part Three

Part Three introduces two activists who are struggling with the entangled nature of neoliberal practices. Both candidly discuss tactics for resistance and activism, including education, the legal system, organising and using the occupation of physical space.

Chapter 6
Interview with Annette Sykes – Blunting the System: The Personal Is the Political

Chapter 7
Interview with Teanau Tuiono – We Are Everywhere

6

Blunting the System:
The Personal Is the Political

Interview with Annette Sykes

Annette Sykes is a lawyer and activist who has worked on a range of significant cases and projects and has a long involvement with numerous groups resisting neoliberalism. She was interviewed in Rotorua in January 2006 by Maria Bargh.

What would you include in a definition of Māori resistance to neoliberalism?
The term neoliberalism, for me, has a specific context and a general application, because the values that it promotes are those Western values based on the fundamental beliefs that people, the power over life, birth and death can be exploited, and that it is alright to accumulate power within elite, small groups who can then determine priorities for a whole community, a whole nation, a whole region. The answer to the question for me though within a Māori context is best illustrated in the debate between the rūnanga corporatism of tribal organisations of recent times versus the upholding of traditional tribal values and way of life practices as undertaken on our marae. Many of our marae are under enormous threat, with the erasure of those values in the modern context occurring at an alarming rate by the substitution of our values system with one that sees no worth in tikanga, no worth in our laws and no worth in our status as tangata whenua. This is something in my experience which is a common consequence of

the adoption of neoliberal practices within communities and the pressures of migration to urban lifestyles that our people have been coerced into.

So when you ask me what would I include in a definition of Māori resistance, such a process must ensure a Māori resistance at those many specific levels that neoliberalism operates to distort or destroy. For instance, globalisation and neoliberalism promotes the substitution of foods and the consumption of fast foods for the nutrition and knowledge that was maintained by what we grew. So at the most basic level, Māori resistance to that is not to go to McDonald's and KFC, and lately with the threat of things like the Bird Flu pandemic, to reinstitute traditional tribal gardens so thus I am encouraging my children to look at growing their own food using traditional Māori food harvesting practices.

In any definition of Māori resistance, for me it must come back to personal commitment to change right through to a political commitment to challenge the inculcation of those neoliberal values into our modern Māori institutions, including direct challenges on corporate elites, which are really the living icons of this philosophy, and challenges too to the government agencies and bureaucrats that corporate elites bribe or co-opt to promote the liberal notions that the monster of globalisation promotes.

I think neoliberalism is a better term than globalisation because globalisation has been manipulated in many minds and, for me, doesn't really encompass the kinds of insidious activities and consequences that neoliberalism has brought to New Zealand since the 1980s. Although if you go back, the beginnings of it, the ideas it promotes, were being planted after the Second World War with the establishment of the United Nations.

Another thing that I would talk about in terms of resistance is that, as a mother, you've got to be creative in your education strategies. One of the good things about rugby for my kids is that they have actually clicked on that food is the key to well-being in rugby. So I have used that kind of thing to teach the kids how to look at health. The Māori rugby coach and the Sevens coach actually spend a lot of time with Māori boys talking about diet, and that's a resistance strategy to neoliberalism. But it can be a difficult one because, of course, that whole world within which that sporting culture lives is the modern opiate of our people as well and operates to subvert Māori culture with the promise of the pot of gold at the end of the rugby corporate rainbow. The rugby contract world can easily also be the beginning of the death of our kids' commitment to our way of life because they go into that kind of middle-class environment where they promote privatisation to exploit the very talent of our young people. The greater the contracts, the more money one earns, and that of itself often distances our people from the very values that people like Matt Te Pou are actually trying to develop and revitalise in Māori rugby teams, which is that if you want to be healthy you don't drink Coke, you do what your tupuna did: walk 20 miles a day and eat seafood, promote whanaungatanga a modern collegiality and loyalty in all you do. Really simple messages, really important things, but they can create a culture of resistance too to the bad things and numbness of individualism that Western capitalism is introducing to our people.

Another thing is that we need to create collective realities of meaning for whānau and hapū in the modern context. The marae are empty except at tangi or birthdays. I live at a marae. So we have got to find ways to get our kids to collectivise. Waka ama is providing some of that opportunity still for a certain kind of sporty person – kapa haka too provides an environment for the practice of our values but again, there is this group of Māori that just seems to move between those pastimes. And that's what worries me; there isn't enough thought on how we can modernise collectivism so that it becomes relevant for all of our people. One of the good suggestions that I thought was made at Te Wānanga o Aotearoa was that we should establish what they called community-based centres on marae, where we can access free computers so we have free technology, and they have on the servers access to some Māori written material around philosophies and practices of relevance to young people, which is so hard to access in these small communities that I tend to dwell, and so that's a resistance strategy too. And that's one thing that the Tino Rangatiratanga website did for us — enabled us to look clearly at a website that educated and promoted strategies for change amongst and between ourselves as Māori.[1]

The other thing too is you've got to promote direct action rather than passive action, and how do you do that in communities? One of the things that I've found very successful around Rotorua, because we always have good marches here on issues of concern, is that you pick a local issue so a whole community gets revived in planning actions to deal with the particular matter. You've got to go from passive to active, but you've also got to look at ways to bring people together that build on existing values, that enable whānau to say that it's alright to be different. It is alright to disagree with the mainstream. That's one of the problems that I have with Rūnanga and Trust Boards, Te Arawa especially, they struggle with this notion of being different to Pākehā corporate citizens and want to copycat their behaviours rather than set themselves apart. And so they are very much caught up in government-created permissive contexts designed around profit margins rather than whānau and hapū well-being, and they expend enormous resources to do so.

At the end of the day Māori resistance is about us surviving as tangata whenua, and it's as basic as that. Our survival as tangata whenua is under threat in so many different ways and contexts, and neoliberalism is one of its deepest causes so we as tangata whenua have to look to our own histories and vehicles of decision-making, our own kawa, if we want real and enduring change.

What kinds of resistance activities have you been involved in?

Just about every kind, some legal and some criminal. When I think back on it, most times they were activities that I had felt some special comfort with. The first one of prominence here in Rotorua was during the Springbok tour, and I was pushing the babies in the pram while the Red Squad was coming out of the airport, and Tame Iti and others were getting arrested. We cared for our children, I was seventeen or eighteen, and I watched everyone else get batoned, and I thought, 'My God, this can't be right.' So from that very first experience, I thought, 'No, this can't be right.' Rather than be paralysed by the fear of this, it actually catalysed me into finding ways to resist what I knew was wrong.

Since then, I've got a much more acute analysis of things, mainly through occupations of land and petitions that I was involved with during the Māori language revival of the 1970's and 1980's and through observing the operations of things like Asia Pacific Economic Cooperation (APEC) and writing speeches that challenge the right of private interests to come here and be treated as a priority over tangata whenua interests around this race for the protection of resources. So my involvement in resistance activities has seen participation right through to travelling internationally to decry the Commonwealth Heads of Government Meeting (CHOGM) in Scotland, and going to Geneva and protesting there as part of the Peoples' Global Action movement.

You have been involved in claims to the Waitangi Tribunal on behalf of people in Tuhoe. In what ways do you see the issues facing Tuhoe as connected to global patterns of neoliberal colonisation/recolonisation?

I have been very privileged to have been involved in the claims for Tuhoe. Sir John Turei called a group together, Tame Iti was the other person who was leading it with the late Tom Winitana, and we ended up acting for twenty-nine claimant groups, which represented five of the valleys of the Urewera and with enormous support from the peoples of Tuhoe themselves.

One of the things I hated, though, was the impotence of the Waitangi Tribunal process itself. It just about killed me to observe how the process becomes ineffective as a result of Crown manipulation. People put a lot of stock into that process that's essentially been established by the Crown and controlled in its effectiveness by Crown funding. And I actually think in hindsight that the process is doing enormous violence because of the hopes that get shattered not by the Tribunal but by the Crown's contempt of the Tribunal's decisions. During the course of the

Tuhoe hearings, settlements were negotiated by Ngāti Awa and the Crown and Te Arawa and the Crown that Tuhoe had interests in. And the way the Crown manipulated it, they masked themselves from the reality of the divisions they created and operated so that they don't even recognise those things like whakapapa that was strained between these groups, so there's deep pain amongst our people and deep rifts created. It's as bad as the Māori Land Court decisions of last century that we are arguing are in breach of the Treaty and I can't ever forget that.

It's the ultimate contradiction too in this whole process that I'm participating daily within something that is described, quite properly, as a toothless tiger. We as lawyers and advocates for our people identify and can prove injustice but what for? To uncover our history, to educate ourselves as much as anything, but also to seek justice from a system that, of itself, can't deliver justice because it is actually perpetuating injustices while we proceed with valid claims. I didn't like it. I find it deeply compromising and often soul destroying.

Having said that, I wonder all the time what is to be my role in life? I pay allegiance to the Crown to practise as a lawyer. So what therefore is my role? Is it just part of the bourgeoisie propping up the ancillary apparatus that forms the state? So why do I do it? Inevitably I come back to the view because the system has got to be blunted against our people.

One of my dreams, while I've still got lots of energy, is that I want to re-establish our own justice systems. I want to recover our own mediation processes, particularly among whānau. The Family Court particularly is where all our people are going, and I really want to help reduce this violence that occurs in whānau as a consequence of stress, not having resources, and the processes of colonisation that are really felt acutely at that level. I want to devote time in my life to restoring the status of women as decision makers of respect in whānau and hapū and as taonga for our people in the lives of our communities. I want our children to be respected and looked after as the future leaders of tomorrow they are and I want our people to be determining how we protect those values in times of whānau crisis and upset so that the dignity of our whakapapa can provide the baseline for solutions in these interpersonal and interwhānau dispute processes.

You were invited to be a prosecutor at the Hong Kong World Trade Organisation meeting in 2005 to prosecute the World Trade Organisation. Do you see the legal system as having the ability to challenge neoliberalism? That is, can the legal system be used to stop rather than support the market mechanism governing peoples?

Yes, I was invited to be a prosecutor to prosecute the WTO, but I couldn't go. However, the prosecution opportunity was amazing because it was looking at the whole question of food sustainability in the South-East Asia-Pacific region, and the fact that all the grains are now substituted by four or five dominant strains of rice or wheat. They used that particular example to highlight how in Burma, Thailand and even here, we are being dominated through the limit of our food choices by this construct of neoliberalisation. I was going to work with a range of activists and great lawyers – because you feel isolated sometimes – and then there were all these indigenous women coming from as far away as Mongolia and right through the region to tell their stories. They were all going to give a testimony to three judges, and I was going to prosecute the WTO for their policies that permitted this stuff … Monsanto going everywhere it's going and looking at policies of WTO and whether that was about promoting well-being and basic human rights or profit for big multinationals.

What that prosecuting tribunal did wasn't so much about effecting change, but about educating people of the realities of what is going on. There was an amazing testimony I read from Thailand about how the flooding and the dams there have created a cultural genocide of their traditional foods. And I learnt too who benefits from the dams? All these big companies from France and America. And their water – they have to end up buying water, their irrigation systems aren't working. And not only that, the dams and flooding have caused major disruption of their food sources.

One of the things I've long advocated is that we need a hui about Māori development that maybe puts 'us' against 'them', the corporates monopolies against small whānau and hapū. But we need to take the World Social Forum and bring it back to Aotearoa and have a Māori Social Forum. We need to bring in those advocates of capitalism and participants of Western capitalistic models who are actually exploiting our resources to death, like the fisheries, to actually sit down and have a debate with those of us who see value in the protection and practice of knowledge that has sustained for thousands of years.

I think it is going to be a really amazing time in the next twenty years. I actually think Aotearoa/New Zealand is going to evolve quite significantly to achieve the independence that we as Māori want and dream for in the next twenty years. It's going to be achieved through a lot of strategies – intermarriage, education, tribal re-organisation, control of our own media and a whole lot of other korero that is going to take place in whānau, hapū and iwi – because the realities of urbanisation, the scarcity of resources, the processes of death that colonisation would invoke on our traditions and our laws are going to require us to look at the revival and the creation of collectives that are born on common values, and I think that's going to be an amazing time. I also think in the Pacific we're going to be supported by our relations from Te Moana Nui a Kiwa, and they are going to need us as we need them to help preserve their ways of life.

I want a small wānanga of writers and dreamers to come together, but I also want activist training camps of the kind I attended when Phillipe Franchet was here in the 1980s, which brought groups of people together to analyse, through simple techniques, what's happening in their lives. Because quite often you haven't got the opportunity to do that. And, most importantly, not to just look at what is happening because of the forces of colonisation but also to look at ways to change that.

Education was our focus then, organisation now or tribal reorganisation now, with activist wānanga as the catalyst for our next phase for liberation. I'm hopeful that this will happen through a revolution of the hearts and minds being planted in a generation of instilled Kaupapa Māori beliefs. And that's not something I dared might be possible in my youth; it's happening.

Notes

1   Tino Rangatiratanga website: www.aotearoa.wellington.net.nz (accessed 9/1/2007).

7

We Are Everywhere

Interview with Teanau Tuiono

Teanau Tuiono is an activist who has been involved in a range of resistance activities against neoliberalism. He has been instrumental in a number of groups that maintain connections between Māori and international activist movements. He was interviewed by Maria Bargh in Wellington in October 2005.

How would you define Māori resistance or Māori activism?

I don't think it's Māori resistance or Māori activism as such, but it's actually a Māori response to a whole lot of kaupapa or issues, like tino rangatiratanga. So for me, Māori activism centres around what Māori people want to achieve in this whole korero about tino rangatiratanga. So the question would be, what do you think tino rangatiratanga is? For me, tino rangatiratanga is a dynamic concept within Māori society. Tino rangatiratanga is about recognising that original resistance, from those early times in the 1800s, and it is a process that has evolved over a period of time to this present day so that tino rangatiratanga has now become a movement in itself, based on all that historical activity. For it to be relevant for the here and now, it's got to be contextualised, not only in that historical time but, more importantly I think, in the context of resistance in the last forty or fifty years.

The period of the 1970s to the 1980s were a crucial time in Aotearoa for Māori. We could have taken a big fall if it wasn't for the actions of the Māori activists at that time organising days of actions around Waitangi Day, land occupations and the concentrated effort of Māoridom to revitalise the Māori language.

In the 1990s and also the 2000s Māori activism needs to evolve and develop as well. The issues are different. We are not only challenging colonisation, that is, the impact of colonisation or British imperialism on our society; we now have to consider neo-colonisation or new colonisation, which is the colonisation of companies through neoliberal policies. I think the old activism of the 1970s and 1980s no longer applies in this brave new world. There will always be a need for indigenous only spaces to organise and consider the challenges of these issues, and it is equally important that there be non-indigenous spaces for Pākehā and other non-indigenous groups to consider Treaty issues and the like. But we also need to think of other spaces to organise. Neoliberalism impacts Māori and non-Māori and in order for us to be successful in dealing with this particular set of issues it makes sense to build a critical mass of people who can approach the kaupapa from as many perspectives as possible. The binary or bicultural model of organising Māori activism is outdated and there are other ways of organising that still retain the independent and autonomous indigenous voice.

How do you think Māori directly resist neoliberalism in Aotearoa?

One of the things that Māori people do – when you're focussing on kaupapa Māori because it's something about ourselves, about where we're from, and it's very local and specific – is that we'll tend to resist things that will be detrimental to that particular way of life, culture or language. Neoliberalism is definitely a threat to that – it's trying to McDonald's-ify everything. So in that sense, the retention of Māori language, for example, whether people involved in that kaupapa want it or not, or even perceive of it as resisting, is a resistance of that general trend of global monoculturalism.

Let's revitalise our language, culture and all that sort of thing, kei te pai. But then, let's also recognise that globalisation is here and exists in a lot of different forms, and there are many other forms that we can use to connect with people who are struggling against exactly the same bodies, like the World Trade Organisation (WTO). It would be strategic for us to actually make connections with those people. For example, one of the good things about the Peoples' Global Action against 'Free' Trade and the World Trade Organisation (PGA) has been the global days of action. You'll get people – Indian farmers, indigenous peoples in Latin America, Māori people here in Aotearoa, people in Australia – protesting against neoliberal globalisation on the same day. That's a really powerful statement when you've got that sort of human diversity coming together on a kaupapa.

I think one of the major problems with the global days of action was September 11, 2001. Globalisation was the new sexy movement, and it was happening all over the place, but then all of a sudden, it just dropped dead. And that's because of what happened on September 11. I think that had a ripple effect across the whole planet, because of the way that dissent is put out there. All protesters are now seen as terrorists.

I think the problem with the PGA network is that it's really, really grassroots. And what I mean by grassroots is that it's got no money. And it's really difficult to put up a whole lot of opposition when the WTO's got money falling out of its offices, and the people who are resisting globalisation haven't got two cents to rub together.

We have seen Pākehā activists incorporating international tactics in their protests, such as clowning. Have you noticed examples of this in Māori actions?

I like this idea of transforming spaces, where streets become not only places of protest but also places of performance, we are after all living in the MTV generation which is saturated with tv/radio/dvd/ipods. Being able to break people out of the matrix of modern life to confront the issues is what activists need to do. Perhaps using ideas like Reclaim the Streets which had a huge impact internationally. From the beginning they were anti-roading protests with a strong emphasis on transforming spaces, where streets became playgrounds and walls became art galleries.

A lot of Māori demonstrations and land occupations are like that. For example, at a protest against the building of a prison at Ngawha we staged a protest at the Department of Corrections here in Wellington, it started off when we entered the building, and we had a karanga. Then we went in and did a haka and had some korero. And in that particular instance, we had transformed that space from a crutty old department office into a Māori space, just by our actions, by using our language and culture to reclaim that particular sort of space. And a lot of land occupations are like that. Pakaitore is classic. There was a park – now it's a marae!

The most recent example of a space transformed that I had the privilege of attending was the re-enactment of the urupatu by Tuhoe in 2005, where they had people on horseback, half naked warriors, a gun shot pōwhiri, and burning cars. Love it or hate it, it made an impact, in fact they were still whingeing about it in Parliament months after the event.

Māori people have a long history of doing that, even longer than Reclaim the Streets. One of the powerful forms of protest is to capture a space and transform it into something else. When that happens, it's a primo thing because dressing up as clowns, a lot of Māori don't dig that. One of the things I learnt from Prague and the way that they approached taking down the World Bank and IMF meeting was recognising that you don't have to try to all get on board the same waka.

All the different groups at a protest should come to an agreement on where the various schools of thought are and work on what you can in common. And all the things you can't work on in common, you come to some sort of agreement, where you can, not to get in anyone's way. But if you must come to some sort of conflict, then plan it out a bit. The media is now the battle ground for the hearts and minds of the people, and the tools are cellphones/internet/digital cameras/ etc...

The thing about Third World indigenous movements is that they're actually a lot more organised than we are. They're actual organisations, and they've got non-governmental organisations as well that go to the United Nations and make interventions and cover that particular level. This is what we need to be doing, we need to operate on as many levels as possible working towards a vision of what we think Tino Rangatiratanga could be.

Are we winning?
No, we're on the back foot. But I think what needs to continue to happen is this whole process of up-skilling. That takes time and resources, and it takes people with the know-how.

At the end of the day, people make their own minds up. But the problem is will they make their minds up with the best amount of information in front of them? That's the problem. The best knowledge and the best information are not in front of everyone. Most Māori that want to do something positive for our people rely to some extent on money from the Government, whether it's as a lawyer working on Tribunal claims, or a Hauora organisation or even as a teacher, people literally cannot afford to bite the hand that feeds them. As an activist you need to be as economically independent as possible which of course is not easy and is the reason you don't see Māori activism offered at many career evenings for our rangatahi. Independent resourcing is needed to carry these issues forward so that campaigns can be thought out strategically, and have, not only short-term strategies, but also mid-term to long-term strategies. Greenpeace does this, and so do many of our indigenous brothers and sisters in the Americas. Why not Māori?

Part Four

Part Four deals with the expressions of resistance manifested against the forced inclusion of Māori in international economic spheres, as well as the use of international human rights spheres to draw connections with other indigenous peoples. Maria Bargh's chapter explores the neoliberal practices and assumptions involved in the negotiation and signing of neoliberal trade agreements by successive governments. Māori resistance to these agreements, she argues, is framed in terms of the need for constitutional change. Claire Charters examines Māori interactions at the United Nations and the successes and drawbacks that Māori encounter as they attempt to have domestic issues addressed in an international arena. Moana Jackson highlights the parallels between Māori and other indigenous peoples' experiences of colonisation and neoliberalism as a new form of colonisation.

Chapter 8
Maria Bargh – A Small Issue of Sovereignty

Chapter 9
Claire Charters – Māori and the United Nations

Chapter 10
Moana Jackson – Globalisation and the Colonising State of Mind

8

A Small Issue of Sovereignty

Maria Bargh

In recent years, the New Zealand government has increased the number of trade agreements that they are negotiating and signing. Their focus has changed significantly from negotiating agreements largely through institutions such as the World Trade Organisation (WTO), with multiple countries, to conducting these negotiations with individual countries or pairs of countries.

The difficulty for Māori within this context is that neoliberal trade agreements encourage policies that support and give rights to large corporations over the very resources that Māori are seeking. The 2006 Trans-Pacific Strategic Economic Partnership (Trans-Pacific) provides an apt example of these neoliberal trade agreements, their content and the predominant mode within which they are negotiated.

The arguments of Māori resisting neoliberal trade agreements are inextricable from accompanying calls for constitutional change and the reaffirmation of tino rangatiratanga. The further embedding of neoliberalism through the signing of neoliberal trade agreements will be subverted, these Māori argue, if there is an overhaul of New Zealand's current constitutional arrangements.

The stepping-stone approach

The Labour Government is currently pursuing a number of bilateral and trilateral neoliberal trade agreements.[1] In the last few years, bilateral and trilateral agreements have increasingly been their focus as challenges from developing countries about inequalities, not only in negotiations within institutions like the WTO, but also regarding the negative consequences of these types of trade agreements on the environment and the well-being of people, have seen negotiations in the WTO slow significantly. The most efficient way, therefore, for neoliberal trade policies to be extended across countries is through a stepping-stone process. Negotiating neoliberal trade agreements country by country eventually has the same effect of embedding these policies. In addition, the process of embedding neoliberal practices is facilitated by these trade agreements, which contain the same central components.

Neoliberal trade agreements usually first include an emphasis on companies or investors, and what rights are available to them.[2] They subsequently have three central features. The first is an emphasis on maintaining a 'level playing field', where local companies and companies from elsewhere are to be treated in the same manner. This is called 'national treatment'. The focus on a supposedly level playing field is also extended to countries; if a new agreement is created with another country, it cannot be accorded special treatment above and beyond the treatment given to countries with whom agreements have already been made. This is called 'most favoured nation status'. Finally, all these kinds of neoliberal trade agreements decree that once neoliberal reforms have been initiated, they must be continued. That is, even if a range of sectors are left out initially, such as education, they will need to be included eventually.[3]

The central features of neoliberal trade agreements also have the ability to be enforced. They are not like United Nations reports, which simply have moral or embarrassment value. The WTO, for example, has the ability to impose trade sanctions on countries if they do not abide by the rules.[4]

The Crown claims that Māori benefit from and have their rights protected under neoliberal trade agreements. The benefits to Māori, they argue, accrue in the same way that they do for all New Zealand companies or consumers, either through increases in exports, or through access to cheaper imported goods.[5] Protections for Māori, they suggest, are contained in Treaty clauses. These clauses were not in fact government initiatives, but came after intense pressure from Māori in the past few years. [6] It remains to be seen how the use of Treaty clauses will be impacted upon by moves to delete references to the principles of the Treaty from legislation.

The most recent agreements, such as the Singapore Closer Economic Partnership, Thailand Closer Economic Partnership, and Trans-Pacific Strategic Economic Partnership, have Treaty clauses. The generic Treaty clause states that:

> ... nothing in this Agreement shall preclude the adoption by Aotearoa New Zealand of measures it deems necessary to accord more favourable treatment to Māori in respect of matters covered by this Agreement including in fulfilment of its obligations under the Treaty of Waitangi.[7]

This clause is limited, however, given that it is left up to the government of the day to determine how it might best fulfil its obligations under the Treaty, which in the past has tended to be at a rather minimal level.[8] A Treaty clause is also not equivalent to Māori, independently from the Crown, and as a party to Te Tiriti o Waitangi being involved in the negotiation and decision making regarding these agreements. An independent decision-making position for Māori in the negotiation of these agreements might go some way towards acknowledging tino rangatiratanga in these cases.

Neoliberal trade agreements have a clear impact on the ability of Māori to reassert or have recognition of tino rangatiratanga. For example, the Trade Related Aspects of Intellectual Property Rights Agreement (TRIPS) encourages the commodification of intellectual and cultural property; that is, it encourages the buying and selling of these properties, making it more difficult for Māori to maintain customary law around these properties and rights. This opens up mātauranga Māori to be bought and sold or misappropriated by foreign companies, and this is included in the Waitangi Tribunal claim WAI 262, discussed by Maui Solomon in Chapter Four.

The TRIPS regime benefits corporations that aim to make money by owning resources, such as seeds and knowledge about medicines, which are all vital to communal survival, but which corporations see merely as commodities to buy and sell for profit. Big corporations are able to pay for establishing patents or trademarks and are able to pay legal fees to defend them. In contrast, most indigenous peoples simply do not have access to those kinds of resources.[9]

The continued entrenchment of market policies in the education sector, including through free trade agreements, also undermines iwi desires to promote whare wānanga and mātauranga Māori. The principles embedded in neoliberal trade agreements, such as not being able to treat local companies differently from foreign ones, can be seen in relation to whare wānanga. The fundamental neoliberal rules about the government not limiting the number of providers in the education sector are included in these kinds of neoliberal trade agreements, and may impact upon Māori in the future. Under the Trans-Pacific Strategic Economic Partnership, the New Zealand Government has reserved the right to adopt or maintain any measure with respect to services, including public education.[10] It is unclear, however, what kinds of institutions this might cover, as the government continues to promote strong connections between private and public educational institutions. If a wānanga was deemed to be beyond the definition of public education, then, for example, Singaporean or Chilean companies could not be prevented by the government from establishing wānanga, under the terms set out in the Trans-Pacific Strategic Economic Partnership. The intellectual and cultural property regime created under the TRIPS could subsequently further enforce this tradability of mātauranga Māori.

The Trans-Pacific Strategic Economic Partnership Agreement

The Trans-Pacific Strategic Economic Partnership (Trans-Pacific), a neoliberal trade agreement signed by the New Zealand Government in 2005 with Brunei, Chile and Singapore, provides an apt illustration of the interconnectedness of government agendas for Māori and long-standing neoliberal attitudes towards indigenous peoples. The claimed benefits for Māori from the Trans-Pacific further lock Māori into a framework conducive to extending the market into areas of the community previously governed in other ways. This significantly reduces the ability of Māori to choose different modes of governance, and restricts tino rangatiratanga. In addition, the process by which the Trans-Pacific was negotiated and signed, with relatively little Māori input, reflects standard neoliberal processes, and is inextricable from the general failure of government to recognise tino rangatiratanga or the position of hapū and iwi as parties to Te Tiriti.

The Crown argued that the Trans-Pacific would benefit New Zealand generally, because it would enable increased exports to the countries involved through 'dynamic productivity gains resulting from improvements in competition', and would 'create opportunities'.[11] Prue Hyman and Jane Kelsey have provided significant critiques of the fallacy of these claims. For example, they have highlighted the fact that tariffs on New Zealand goods to these countries before the signing of the agreement were already negligible, making the claimed need for it redundant. They argue that the main beneficiary, particularly with regard to increased exports to Chile, will be the New Zealand dairy company Fonterra, whose interests should not be confused with New Zealand's national interests. [12]

Embedding neoliberal corporate values

One of the government's central claims about the benefits that Māori would derive from the Trans-Pacific was that it would support 'indigenous business links'. This followed on from their initial analysis that it would benefit 'indigenous cultural links'.[13] In their early documentation, the Ministry of Foreign Affairs and Trade (MFAT) argued that the primary benefits for Māori were the potential cultural links between Māori and, specifically, the Mapuche people of Chile and the people of Rapa Nui (also known as Easter Island, which is a Chilean territory). In their later documentation, the wording changed, and 'indigenous business links' were identified as the primary benefits.[14]

The alleged benefits for Māori through indigenous business links are suggested by MFAT as potentially occurring in 'tourism, agriculture and fisheries', which are highlighted as areas that will 'open opportunities for the transfer of ideas and expertise through business co-operation and joint ventures'[15] between indigenous businesses. Anecdotal evidence suggests that there are currently no substantial indigenous business links between Māori, Mapuche and the people of Rapa Nui, and it is unclear whether the Mapuche or people of Rapa Nui would have the resources to facilitate such links, particularly given the levels of poverty in some of these communities.[16]

The shift in MFAT language from cultural to business links, in relation to the benefits accruing to Māori, is noteworthy when placed in the context of neoliberal assumptions about Māori. Neoliberal advocates assume that in order to manage Māori authorities, institutions and businesses, market training is required, or else cultural factors will encourage unsavoury practices such as corruption. Yet actual corruption in the marketplace is often ignored by neoliberal advocates.[17] Market training would involve making indigenous peoples into self-maximising individuals who prioritise maximising profit ahead of other concerns, and would fundamentally change the nature of the relationships Māori have with tribal organisations. These attitudes are evident in government practices towards Māori in the Treaty settlements process, through their encouragement of corporate and corporate-type governance entities prior to settlement.[18]

Encouraging indigenous business links is non-threatening to the state, as the 'business citizen' matches the concept of 'civilised citizen'. While the Trans-Pacific agreement is primarily economic, it would be scarcely imaginable that the New Zealand or Chilean governments would encourage political links between Māori, Mapuche and the people of Rapa Nui. Such political links would undoubtedly involve strengthening opposition to the current marginalised status of indigenous peoples and indigenous rights in these countries. Given the New Zealand government's stance on the Declaration on the Rights of Indigenous Peoples, in which they have refused to accept the right of indigenous peoples to self-determination, clearly those sorts of links would not be acceptable.[19] For neoliberal advocates, therefore, encouraging indigenous peoples, and in this case Māori, to be business beings is part of the so-called civilising process.[20]

To simply suggest, however, that Māori participation in business can purely be viewed as part of neoliberal practices and agendas would be to leave the argument incomplete, and would deny Māori agency in this process. Māori business people are involved with neoliberal practices and agendas in multiple ways, including rejecting them and supporting diverse political economies and multiple forms of production and trade (not simply neoliberal ones), as well as by wholeheartedly embracing them.[21] What is crucial to consider, even for those Māori engaged in diverse ways in neoliberal practices and agendas, are the long-standing Western beliefs that underpin neoliberalism, and what consequences these have for Māori values and beliefs. It is insufficient for neoliberal advocates to reject Māori ways of doing things simply because they are contrary to neoliberal agendas.

Embedded neoliberal practices

The Trans-Pacific deal is similar to a series of other neoliberal trade agreements, not simply in terms of the policies and principles that underpin it, but also in terms of the process by which it was negotiated, with little public input and marginalisation of critical voices.[22] Consultation of any kind with Māori was negligible, let alone at a level that would recognise Māori tino rangatiratanga or Māori as a party to Te Tiriti o Waitangi.

In terms of consultation with Māori outside government, the Federation of Māori Authorities (FOMA) was the only Māori organisation to be consulted. It is listed as having made a submission; however, it is not specified if FOMA provided a written submission.[23] FOMA is a Māori business network that aims to promote Māori economic development by supporting Māori authorities with a focus on 'land related development and the primary industries'.[24] There is no record of what perspective FOMA provided in their consultation or submission. The Ministry of Foreign Affairs and Trade (MFAT) National Interest Analysis simply notes that they were consulted and made a submission.[25] It is unclear at what level this consultation took place; did it simply involve a conversation, or were FOMA member groups contacted? Given that FOMA is a business network, it could reasonably be expected that it may not necessarily have been in complete opposition to the agreement. Either way, it is not sufficient for one particular perspective only to be accepted as supposedly representing all Māori.

If we examine the kinds of precedents that have been established in law and in conventions with regard to consultation, it becomes apparent that the conduct of the government, and MFAT in particular, on the Trans-Pacific falls short in this regard. The Wellington Airport case[26] established a number of principles regarding genuine consultation, including that it is meaningful only when 'parties are provided with sufficient information to enable them to make "intelligent and useful responses" and is undertaken with an open mind'.[27] The Waitangi Tribunal has also established a number of principles regarding consultation with Māori, including that the Crown has a duty to consult as a way to demonstrate good faith; consultation must also involve a diverse range of Māori groups, provide sufficient time, preferably be face to face, and there must be an active protection of Māori rights.[28]

In the case of the Trans-Pacific deal, these principles were not followed. At this point, we need to ask what the significance of this failure to consult represents. Is this an isolated case, or is this the standard mode of operation in the negotiation of international neoliberal agreements and treaties? The disjuncture between the precedents and principles established in law and the way successive governments behave indicates that governments have some distance to go in order to adhere adequately to Te Tiriti o Waitangi. This lack of consultation is perceived by some as one of the reasons why constitutional change is required to genuinely honour Te Tiriti.

Constitutional change – intertwined with resistance to neoliberal trade agreements

Māori opposition to neoliberal agreements is intertwined with campaigns for constitutional change, which might uphold Te Tiriti and provide Māori with a stronger role in national decision making and, therefore, an ability to reject neoliberal agendas. Calls for constitutional change by Māori have a long history. The calls, workshops and educational campaigns were particularly prevalent around the foreshore and seabed issue in 2003 and 2004.[29]

At meetings regarding the foreshore and seabed and constitutional change, many proposals and models built upon those that had been discussed at meetings called by Hepi Te Heuheu in 1995 and 1996.[30] Even earlier calls for constitutional change stem from the 1840s. These are well documented elsewhere; they include numerous letters, petitions, submissions, deputations to England, activities of the Māori parliament, occupations, hikoi and war.[31] These activities have all taken place over long periods of time in an attempt to engage the Crown on issues of land, rangatiratanga and Crown assumptions of sovereignty.[32]

Calls for constitutional change were reinforced by the report of the United Nation's Special Rapporteur on the Situation of Human Rights and Fundamental Freedoms of Indigenous Peoples, which was released in April 2006. The Special Rapporteur, Rudolfo Stavenhagen, recognised the need for constitutional reform to 'clearly regulate the relationship between the Government and Māori on the basis of the Treaty of Waitangi and the internationally recognized right of all peoples to self-determination'.[33]

Māori resistance to neoliberal trade agreements

One of the central connections between calls for constitutional change and open resistance to neoliberal trade agreements is the emphasis that Māori groups place on Te Tiriti. The central principles inherent in Te Tiriti, including the reaffirmation of tino rangatiratanga, are perceived as the key reasons why the government should not be able to sign neoliberal trade agreements.

Tino rangatiratanga is often understood as a translation for the term 'self-determination'. According to Māori understandings, tino rangatiratanga has particular connotations and rules attached to it, relating to mana whenua, mana moana, mana tangata and Te Tiriti.[34] Self-determination also has specific rules attached to it, particularly in the framework of the United Nations. The International Covenant on Civil and Political Rights (ICCPR) and the International Covenant on Economic, Social and Cultural Rights (ICESCR), both of which the New Zealand government has signed and ratified, outline the right of all peoples to self-determination.[35] The Declaration on the Rights of Indigenous Peoples highlights that the right of self-determination extends to indigenous peoples, as Claire Charters outlines in her chapter.

During the negotiations of the Multilateral Agreement on Investment (MAI) in 1997 and 1998, an agreement that would make it easier for foreign investors to operate in this country, as well as more rigorously bind governments to their terms, Māori protested at government consultation meetings around the country. Those Māori who rejected the deal highlighted the inappropriateness of the government entering into an international treaty that would give foreign investors rights over the very land and other resources that Māori were already contesting the government for.[36] Due to breaches of Te Tiriti, Māori have to negotiate for the return of resources that, if in private ownership, would not be able to be returned.[37]

The Singapore–New Zealand Closer Economic Partnership Agreement, which proposed, among other things, to support general neoliberal policies 'to liberalise bilateral trade in goods and services and to establish a framework conducive to bilateral investments',[38] and to 'liberate' trade and investment between Singapore and New Zealand, also ignited active protests from tino rangatiratanga advocates.[39] These advocates argued that this agreement would marginalise Māori further by damaging industries where Māori are predominately employed, and that the process by which it was negotiated once again ignored Māori as a party to Te Tiriti.[40]

Many tino rangatiratanga advocates argue that for the Crown to actively uphold Te Tiriti, the government would need to obtain the consent of Māori before any agreements or treaties were entered into. Mason Durie also suggests that in exercising their indigeneity, 'Māori might wish to establish closer relations with many other groups, apart from the Crown, including other indigenous peoples, even to sign treaties with them'.[41] These assertions using Te Tiriti strengthen Moana Jackson's argument that, 'The Treaty is not an illusion of political authority, it is a re-affirmation of the rights of Māori to determine their own lives',[42] and that this includes international relations.

Māori campaigning against neoliberal policies and agendas have also sought support and combined with non-Māori at the local and international level. Significant cooperation has taken place as anarchists, environmentalists, animal rights activists, trade unionists, peace activists and tino rangatiratanga advocates work together and in combination with international movements against neoliberal practices and agendas. Māori representatives have been active participants in international anti-neoliberal forums, such as the Peoples' Global Action Against 'Free' Trade and the World Trade Organisation (PGA), and have adopted various tactics from these forums.[43] Some of these groups support Māori rights associated with tino rangatiratanga and Te Tiriti, while others, such as the PGA, frame Māori issues around broader indigenous rights and resistance to oppression more generally.

Conclusion

The Crown's pursuit of neoliberal trade agreements has serious consequences for Māori. First, these agreements allow for rights to be afforded to big companies, often based outside Aotearoa. The rights afforded to these companies are rights that Māori are struggling to have reaffirmed in a way that accords with Te Tiriti. Secondly, the manner in which the government conducts the negotiation of neoliberal trade agreements is a concern to Māori. Limited or no consultation takes place with Māori. Both of these aspects contribute to limiting Māori tino rangatiratanga, and reflect inherent assumptions underpinning neoliberal practices regarding indigenous peoples. Māori are resisting the continued limiting of tino rangatiratanga by foregrounding tino rangatiratanga and Te Tiriti, and calling for constitutional change to deconstruct the very system that allows neoliberal trade agreements to be entered into in this manner.

It is important to note that while tino rangatiratanga may be limited by government and neoliberal trade agreements, Māori are independently strengthening tino rangatiratanga in all sorts of ways. These include returning land to communal ownership, pursuing development activities that do not subscribe entirely to dominant ways of conducting business, and strengthening practices that reaffirm values and world-views contrary to neoliberal ones.[44] Strengthening local community initiatives, local economies, mātauranga and decision-making processes that neoliberal policies find difficult reasserts tino rangatiratanga by reaffirming the world over which neoliberal policies do not have complete control. The fact that neoliberal practices and agendas do not have complete control means that there is space to create new ways of surviving and thriving.

Notes

1   See examples on the Ministry of Foreign Affairs and Trade website: www.mfat.govt.nz (accessed 26/4/2006).
2   See, for example, trade agreements on the Ministry of Foreign Affairs and Trade website: www. mfat.govt.nz (accessed 9/1/2007).
3   These principles are often referred to as 'National Treatment', 'Most Favoured Nation Status' and 'Rollback' or 'Progressive Liberalisation' respectively. For more on these points, see Walden Bello, *Deglobalization: Ideas for a New World Economy*, London: Zed Books, 2005.
4   See WTO website, 'Understanding the WTO: Settling Disputes', http://www.wto.org/english/ thewto_e/whatis_e/tif_e/disp1_e.htm (accessed 28/4/2006).
5   See, for example, the Ministry of Foreign Affairs and Trade website, www.mfat.govt.nz.
6   Anecdotal evidence suggests this pressure came not simply from consultations with Māori, but also from the Ministry of Māori Affairs, Te Puni Kokiri.
7   *Agreement Between New Zealand and Singapore on a Closer Economic Partnership*, Part 11: General Provisions, Article 74. Ministry of Foreign Affairs and Trade New Zealand website: www.mfat. govt.nz/foreign/regions/sea/singcep5.html (accessed 9/8/2002).
8   An apt example would be the government's perspectives on their responsibilities in the Treaty settlements process.
9   See V. Shiva and R. Holla-Bhar, 'Piracy by Patent: The Case of the Neem Tree', in J. Mander and E. Goldsmith (eds), *The Case Against the Global Economy and For a Turn Toward the Local*, San Francisco: Sierra Club Books, 1996.

10 Trans-Pacific Strategic Economic Partnership Agreement, Ministry of Foreign Affairs and Trade website, http://www.mfat.govt.nz/tradeagreements/transpacepa/transpacsepindex.html (accessed 28/4/2006).

11 Ministry of Foreign Affairs and Trade, 'Trans-Pacific Strategic Economic Partnership Agreement: National Interest Analysis', Wellington: Ministry of Foreign Affairs and Trade, 2005, pp. 9-10.

12 P. Hyman, 'Critique of the Proposed Chile/New Zealand Closer Economic Partnership P3 with Singapore', Wellington: ARENA, 2004; J. Kelsey, Submission to the Foreign Affairs and Trade Select Committee on the Trans-Pacific Strategic Economic Cooperation Agreement, November 2005. Both Hyman and Kelsey also highlighted the significant dangers of a 'negative list'.

13 The Indigenous peoples that government officials were referring to were the Mapuche in Chile and Rapa Nui on the island of Rapa Nui. No mention was made of other Indigenous peoples in these countries and it is unclear why these two groups were selected.

14 Ministry of Foreign Affairs and Trade, 'An Initial Analysis on the Trade and Economic Benefits of Negotiating a "Pacific Three" Closer Economic Partnership Agreement Involving Chile', Ministry of Foreign Affairs and Trade website, www.mfat.govt.nz/foreign/tnd/ceps/cepchilenzsing/chilenzsingcep1.html (accessed 31/5/2005).

15 Ministry of Foreign Affairs and Trade, 2005.

16 Hyman, 2004.

17 See P. Larmour and N. Wolanin (eds), *Corruption and Anti-Corruption*, Canberra: Asia Pacific Press, 2001.

18 Bargh, 2002.

19 Ministry of Foreign Affairs and Trade, 'New Zealand Negotiating Brief on the Draft Declaration on the Rights of Indigenous Peoples', Wellington: New Zealand Government, 1999.

20 See Bargh, 2002; B. Hindess, 'Neo-liberal Citizenship', *Citizenship Studies*, Vol. 6, No. 2, 2002.

21 For a range of these perspectives, see the Hui Taumata Summary of Feedback reports 2005, Hui Taumata website, http://www.huitaumata.maori.nz/ (accessed 10/4/2006).

22 Hyman, 2004.

23 Ministry of Foreign Affairs and Trade, 2005, p. 60.

24 FOMA website, http://www.foma.co.nz/static/about_foma/about_foma.htm (accessed 9/1/2007).

25 Ministry of Foreign Affairs and Trade, 2005.

26 *Wellington International Airport Ltd v Air New Zealand* [1993] 1 NZLR 671.

27 Te Puni Kokiri, *He Tirohanga o Kawa ti te Tiriti o Waitangi: a Guide to the Principles of the Treaty of Waitangi as expressed by the Court and the Waitangi Tribunal*, Wellington: Te Puni Kokiri, 2001a, p. 87.

28 Ibid, p. 90.

29 In 2003, the Court of Appeal ruled that Māori could take claims regarding customary title in the foreshore and seabed to the Māori Land Court. However, the government announced that they would legislate to vest the foreshore and seabed in Crown ownership. Māori overwhelmingly rejected the government's proposals and Bill in numerous ways, including in submissions, a Waitangi Tribunal hearing, direct protest and declarations. Many of the Māori responses highlighted the way that the Bill breached national and international laws and standards. The government ignored Māori and reasserted the supremacy of Parliament by passing the Act and overriding Māori concerns. This highlighted to many Māori the pressing need for constitutional change. See *Attorney-General v Ngati Apa* [2003] 3 NZLR 643; Paeroa Declaration, 12 July 2003 at http://www.converge.org.nz/pma/paeroa.htm#btpd (accessed 28/4/2006). Resolutions from Omaka Hui, 30 August 2003 at http://www.converge.org.nz/pma/in300803.htm (accessed 28/4/2006); Hongoeka Foreshore and Seabed Hui, 18 December 2003, http://www.foma.co.nz/archive/HongoekaForeshoreSeabedHuiResolutions.htm (accessed 28/4/2006); Te Tii Mangonui Ki Te Tai Tokerau Declaration at http://www.terarawa.co.nz/mahi/rm/seabed/seabed_9.htm (accessed 28/4/2006). See also, for example, M. Mutu, 'Submission on the Foreshore and Seabed Bill', Fisheries and Other Sea Related Legislation Select Committee, 2004, http://www.clerk.parliament.govt.nz/content/Select_Committee_Submissions/Fisheries_and_other_Sea

related Legislation Committee/Foreshore and Seabed Bill/M to N/Mutu%20M%200291. pdf (accessed 28/4/2006).

30 See, for example, details of the hui held at Waitangi, July 2005, Crown Forest Rental Trust website, http://www.cfrt.org.nz/storehouse/publications/july05newsletter.asp (accessed 6/9/2005).

31 See, for example, R. Walker, *Ka Whawhai Tonu Matou*, Auckland: Penguin Books, 1990; C. Orange, *The Treaty of Waitangi,* Wellington: Allen and Unwin Port Nicholson Press with assistance from the Historical Publications Branch, Department of Internal Affairs, 1987; A. Harris, *Hikoi: Forty Years of Maori Protest*, Wellington: Huia Publishers, 2004.

32 The question may be whether Te Tiriti should be considered more legally binding. Lawyer Mai Chen has suggested that this could be achieved through a Supreme Court ruling which outlines the limits of Crown kawanatanga and parliamentary sovereignty, and overturns precedent about the need for Te Tiriti to be incorporated into statute before it is legally enforceable. Mai Chen, 'Māori Push Over Treaty May End in Court', *New Zealand Herald*, 27 March 2006.

33 United Nations Special Rapporteur on the situation of human rights and fundamental freedoms of indigenous peoples, 'Indigenous Issues', E/CN.4/2006/78/1dd.3, Economic and Social Council, VI, 84.

34 See I. H. Kawharu (ed.), 1989; M. Durie, 'Tino Rangatiratanga' in M. Belgrave, M. Kawharu and D. Williams (eds), *Waitangi Revisited*, Melbourne: Oxford University Press, 2005.

35 United Nations website, http://www.unhchr.ch/html/menu3/b/a_ccpr.htm (accessed 4/12/2006) and http://www.ohchr.org/english/law/cescr.htm (accessed 1/12/2006). See also Peace Movement Aotearoa, 'Act Now for Indigenous Peoples' Rights' Peace Movement Aotearoa website, http://www.converge.org.nz/pma/in080306.htm (accessed 28/10/2006). Self-determination does have a particular trajectory in international law and a universalised system of human rights and a particular notion of 'self'; however, at a broad level it gets towards my usage of tino rangatiratanga here.

36 Bargh, 2002.

37 For more information with regard to Māori resource management, see M. Kawharu (ed.), *Whenua: Managing Our Resources*, Auckland: Reed, 2002.

38 Part 1, Article 1 (b) of the *Agreement Between New Zealand and Singapore on a Closer Economic Partnership*. See Ministry of Foreign Affairs and Trade website for the full text, http://www.mfat. govt.nz/foreign/regions/sea/singcep.html#Part%201:%20Objectives%20and%20General%20D efinitions (accessed 15/8/2002).

39 Aotearoa Educators [AE!] 'Prague Style Protests to Hit Aotearoa if Singapore Deal Continues', Press Release, 26 September 2000. See also Aotearoa Educators [AE!] 'Potential Threat to Singaporean Investment by Māori', Press Release, 4 August 2000.

40 Aotearoa Educators [AE!] 'Prague Style Protests to Hit Aotearoa if Singapore Deal Continues', Press Release, 26 September 2000.

41 M. Durie, A Framework for Considering Māori Educational Advancement, Opening Address at the Hui Taumata Matauranga, Turangi, Aotearoa New Zealand, 24 February 2001.

42 M. Jackson, 'Comment' in G. McLay (ed.), *Treaty Settlements*, Wellington: New Zealand Institute of Advanced Legal Studies, 1995, p. 157.

43 See PGA website, www.agp.org (accessed 28/4/2006).

44 See, for example, the Tuaropaki Trust, on their website, http://www.tuaropaki.com/home.asp (accessed 5/12/2006).

9

Māori and the United Nations

Claire Charters

This chapter describes both positive and negative phenomena related to Māori and globalisation, based on recent Māori involvement in United Nations (UN) forums. The first positive is that globalisation assists Māori to raise domestic issues at the UN in order to further domestic agendas. The second, and the flip side of the first, is that local issues influence the content of indigenous peoples' global movements and international law advanced at the UN. Thirdly, globalisation has enabled indigenous peoples to pool resources in unique ways to assist each other in advancing both local and shared global objectives, typically to resist states' authority and/or the power of multinational corporations. Fourthly, states and multinational corporations are not the only entities that influence global politics as played out in the UN. Some room exists for indigenous peoples, even though states remain the dominant players.

The first negative is that the heavy influence of global neoliberal economic policy on the UN has been, to some extent, an impediment to indigenous peoples achieving their goals within that forum. Lastly, there are some practical and institutional difficulties facing Māori and other indigenous peoples when participating in the UN, including limited resources and the make-up of the UN system, which reflects entrenched and dominant global power structures.

An overriding theme in this chapter is that globalisation is not confined to the proliferation of neoliberal market policies. It also includes better opportunities for indigenous peoples to coordinate, and the emergence of supranational institutions with some jurisdiction over states, such as the UN, in which indigenous peoples participate. These enable innovative responses to both continuing state control over indigenous peoples, and the very same neoliberal ideas that are often considered the engine of globalisation.[1] Another theme is that indigenous peoples, Māori included, are not neutral in their interaction with the globalised world; they utilise the opportunities provided by globalisation to promote their own interests. However, the positives of globalisation for Māori participating at the UN are, nonetheless, muted by the impact of the dominance of market-driven economic policy internationally, and particularly by the pressure to privatise and exploit indigenous peoples' territories and resources.

In sum, globalisation is a mixed bag for indigenous peoples active in the UN. On the one hand, it presents new challenges, most clearly in the form of commodification of indigenous lands and cultures for corporate exploitation. On the other, it provides indigenous peoples with new opportunities.

It is an appropriate time to consider Māori involvement in the UN. In 2005, there was increased interaction between the two, leading to heightened domestic awareness of UN concern for Māori economic, cultural, political and social well-being. A number of iwi successfully sought criticism of the Foreshore and Seabed Act 2004 (FSA) by the UN Committee on the Elimination of Racial Discrimination (CERD).[2] The UN Special Rapporteur on the Human Rights and Fundamental Freedoms of Indigenous Peoples visited Aotearoa in November 2005, attracting significant public and political attention. Finally, at the very end of 2005, overseas indigenous peoples' representatives, in conjunction with some Māori individuals, raised concerns both in Aotearoa and overseas with New Zealand's proposed amendments to the UN Draft Declaration on the Rights of Indigenous Peoples (now the UN Declaration on the Rights of Indigenous Peoples).[3]

This chapter is written from my personal perspective and does not speak for other Māori and their experiences at the UN.[4] Nonetheless, I hope that the conclusions drawn here have a broader reach.

Indigenous peoples, UN institutions and international law

Indigenous peoples have a history of bringing concerns to international forums, predating contemporary globalisation. For example, the Iroquois Confederacy sought, albeit unsuccessfully, to bring their claims against Canada to the League of Nations in the 1920s.[5] Indigenous peoples have also been an object of Western-centric international law for centuries, in part as a direct result of colonial pursuits. Since at least the 1500s, states and jurists evolved international norms to regulate and, in particular, justify colonisation and subjugation of indigenous peoples.[6]

However, effective spaces for indigenous peoples in international forums have been developed only within the last fifty years, at most. It can be no coincidence that these spaces evolved in an era of increased globalisation. Improved tools to communicate assisted indigenous peoples to present a united indigenous voice, and collectively lobby for international institutional attention.

By 2005, the UN included a number of institutions that focus on indigenous peoples and their rights under international law. Of the bodies that focus exclusively on indigenous peoples, the Working Group on Indigenous Populations is the oldest.[7] Its mandate is to review developments relating to the human rights of indigenous peoples, and to focus on the evolution of those rights. The newest forum is the Permanent Forum on Indigenous Issues, an advisory body to the UN Economic and Social Council, which has the mandate to discuss indigenous issues related to economic and social development, culture, the environment, education, health and human rights.[8] The UN Commission on Human Rights established a working group to elaborate on the Draft Declaration in 1995, in which states and indigenous peoples participate. The Special Rapporteur on the Human Rights and Fundamental Freedoms of Indigenous Peoples has a number of functions, including reviewing states' relationships with indigenous peoples. He is the last in a line of UN special rapporteurs to have the mandate to focus on specific indigenous peoples' issues.[9]

A number of other UN bodies also address indigenous issues, albeit not to the exclusion of other issues. They include the General Assembly, the Economic and Social Council, the Human Rights Council and the United Nations Development Program. The 1992 UN Conference on Environment and Development concentrated on indigenous peoples in the context of the environment.[10]

Indigenous peoples' issues are not raised only at the UN, nor are they exclusively a UN concern. For example, the International Labour Organisation (ILO) monitors ILO Convention 169 on Indigenous and Tribal Peoples. [11] This is the only treaty to deal exclusively with indigenous peoples' rights emanating from an international institution. However, it is currently ratified by only 17 states.[12] The World Bank has a policy on indigenous peoples, and the Convention on Biodiversity includes an article relating to indigenous peoples' traditional knowledge.[13]

International law, a significant amount of which emanates from the UN, provides some protection of indigenous peoples' rights. In particular, indigenous peoples, including Māori, have invoked human rights enshrined in widely ratified treaties, such as the International Covenant on Civil and Political Rights, in both domestic and international forums.[14] Given that indigenous individuals can, in some cases, bring claims against states directly to UN human rights treaty bodies, these can be useful tools in indigenous peoples' armoury against state action in breach of their human rights. However, ILO Convention 169 aside, there is not one international treaty that comprehensively enshrines indigenous peoples' rights as a distinct body of international law.

It is also difficult to argue that a discrete body of indigenous peoples' rights constitutes customary international law.[15] Nonetheless, some specific indigenous peoples' rights are international law. A number of international legal norms have been interpreted to apply to indigenous peoples, including the right to self-determination and the right to culture.[16] The UN Declaration on the Rights of Indigenous Peoples deserves special mention in this regard. As a declaration, it is not binding; however, it does elaborate norms that could well form the basis of international law on indigenous peoples' rights in the future.

Positives of globalisation for Māori participation in the UN

Māori utilisation of international forums to advance domestic agendas

Māori have been able to advance domestic political and legal agendas effectively by participating in UN forums. One of the better examples is the Te Rūnanga o Ngai Tahu, Treaty Tribes Coalition and Taranaki Māori Trust Board complaint to the UN CERD Committee that the Foreshore and Seabed Bill, and later the Foreshore and Seabed Act (FSA), breached the right to freedom from racial discrimination. The outcome of the complaint, a finding by an impartial *international* institution that New Zealand is in breach of human rights, was important *domestically* for a number of reasons. It has been used by both the Māori Party and the Green Party as leverage to galvanise support for amendments for the FSA; it legitimises the massive Māori protest against the FSA; and it embarrasses the government.

What is particularly significant, however, is that the iwi involved in the CERD Committee proceedings were able to achieve outcomes which they simply could not have attained domestically. Given New Zealand's constitutional structure and legal system, Māori could not have had an independent and authoritative institution assess Parliament's compliance with human rights so close to the enactment of offending legislation at home. While New Zealand courts have jurisdiction to consider legislation's consistency with the right to freedom from discrimination, the time required to bring such a claim to fruition is long,[17] and the Waitangi Tribunal does not have the express mandate to assess legislation against human rights. In this sense, a globalised world that includes international institutions provides Māori with avenues to resist state domination that would not otherwise be available. As Sarah Pritchard has pointed out:

> [I]ndigenous peoples have recognised international legal constructions as a resource which can be used to reach out beyond the normative and political boundaries of the State and its law. Increasingly, the search for legal spaces in which indigenous identities can be negotiated and constructed by indigenous peoples themselves has been carried out in international fora and with reference to international norms.[18]

The CERD Committee's FSA decision further illustrates that Māori strategies of resistance can be more multi-pronged and cumulative in an era of globalisation. They can include modes of resistance on the ground, such as protest, and in both international and domestic political and legal spheres. The addition of international avenues to confront objectionable state action adds a unique dimension that can form part of broader and holistic Māori strategies.

Similarly, Māori use of the UN to advance domestic agendas is in itself multi-pronged and cumulative in its own right. For example, prior to the CERD Committee's FSA decision, Māori had made interventions in the Working Group on Indigenous Populations, the Permanent Forum on Indigenous Issues and in negotiations on the Draft Declaration, expressing their objection to the government's foreshore and seabed policies. In an effort to maintain international criticism of the FSA, numerous iwi and hapū representatives also criticised the FSA before the UN Special Rapporteur on Human Rights and Indigenous Peoples.[19]

Māori have also used the UN to progress the tino rangatiratanga movement. It is not uncommon to see tino rangatiratanga expressed and translated as self-determination,[20] a term that has distinct meanings and connotations under international law and in UN forums.[21] In this way, we see Māori utilising a term with global significance to lend additional legitimacy to a domestic platform of resistance to the New Zealand government's assertion of sovereignty over Māori. It is noteworthy that the Māori self-determination vernacular is utilised in a context of increased tribalism and localisation on a global level, for which the phenomenon of globalisation similarly has some responsibility, and which is related to the international self-determination movement. As Pamela Jefferies has noted:

> It is notable that as the world becomes more global and is defined by CNN, the Internet, mobile phones, and McDonald's, there is resurgence in tribalism or states within states. In some states it is represented by a demand by indigenous populations for their rights particularly associated with land, e.g., Aboriginal tribes in Australia, Māori iwi in New Zealand, Karen people in Thailand/Myanmar. In others there is concern to protect traditional group rights from being trampled on in the name of progress, e.g., Indonesia, Philippines, and India. [22]

Māori influence on the international indigenous peoples' rights movements and international law

In the process of advancing domestic agendas by utilising international forums, indigenous peoples have often simultaneously influenced, perhaps sometimes unwittingly, the focus of broader indigenous peoples' rights movements and the content of international legal norms relating to indigenous peoples. Māori have participated instrumentally in this process.

The best example of indigenous peoples' domestic agendas influencing international movements and legal norms is perhaps the UN Declaration on the Rights of Indigenous Peoples itself. The rights expressed in it reflect some indigenous peoples' most pressing domestic concerns, such as self-determination, protection of indigenous peoples' land rights and redress for indigenous peoples' loss of land.[23] Some Māori, such as Moana Jackson, were influential in the drafting of this Declaration. It would seem likely that, in seeking protection of self-determination and land rights in an international instrument, he was inspired by the tino rangatiratanga movement in Aotearoa and the fact of significant Māori loss of land historically.

Māori complaints about domestic issues to international human rights treaty bodies have similarly influenced the evolving content of international law on indigenous peoples' rights. For example, the CERD Committee decision on the FSA consolidates international human rights law on indigenous peoples' land rights. In particular, it clarifies that states breach international obligations if they discriminate in their treatment of indigenous peoples' land rights and non-indigenous peoples' land rights. The CERD Committee's FSA decision builds on earlier CERD Committee decisions on indigenous peoples' rights, instigated by other indigenous peoples' complaints against state action,[24] and its own General Recommendation on Indigenous Peoples.[25]

The communication brought by Api Mahuika to the UN Human Rights Committee in 1992, arguing that the Sealord Fisheries Settlement breached his right to access culture, had a profound impact on the content of indigenous peoples' rights in international law. The Human Rights Committee decision on that communication clarified the important legal principles that indigenous peoples have the right to choose to develop their traditional cultural rights into modern economic activities, and the right to self-determination.[26]

Any benefits of indigenous peoples advancing the international indigenous rights movement by raising domestic issues before UN forums are, therefore, cumulative. Indigenous peoples can now argue that states must not fall below UN and international legal standards upheld by international human rights treaty bodies.

Enhanced coordination between indigenous peoples

Pamela Jefferies points out that:

> The Internet, while allowing mass communication, also allows development of the smallest group into an effective lobby against multinational companies, which are presumed

to oppress their rights, thus adding to the demands of small groupings that they achieve political and religious autonomy in some form of derogation of state power. [27]

The increased opportunities to communicate and travel which are significant components of globalisation have had an infinitely positive impact on some indigenous peoples' ability to pursue both domestic and international agendas, as the recent experience of Māori in UN forums has borne out.

On the international level, many indigenous peoples have been able to coordinate to advance collective goals of greater legal protection of their rights in complex and nuanced ways. On the domestic level, specific indigenous peoples have found strong support from other indigenous peoples for local resistance to governmental action, and this support has been extremely powerful in local and international forums. However, some indigenous peoples from developing countries, where access to tools for communication is less common and finances to travel are not available, have found it difficult to participate in the indigenous peoples' movement in these ways. This issue is discussed below.

Coordinated lobbying by indigenous peoples at an international level was, unsurprisingly, an important catalyst in the UN's establishment of forums exclusively for indigenous peoples, such as the Working Group on Indigenous Populations in 1982. The advent of greater and easier opportunities for communication through email and internet access has only increased the ability of indigenous peoples' groups from different parts of the globe to lobby jointly. A relevant example is the American Indian Law Alliance's (AILA) response to the amendments to the self-determination articles in the Draft Declaration, proposed by New Zealand, Australia and the United States, which were presented to the UN in December 2005.

There were no Māori present in Geneva when New Zealand formally introduced its proposals. However, within minutes of New Zealand's intervention, a representative of AILA had emailed Māori colleagues to report on and criticise New Zealand's proposals, pointing out the need to galvanise Māori resistance to them. Within the next twenty-four hours, AILA, with assistance from some Māori individuals, had drafted and disseminated a press release in New Zealand. It was then published in a number of places, including on a New Zealand-based news website.[28] By the end of the following week, the same AILA representative gave an interview on New Zealand radio, and a statement from numerous Māori criticising New Zealand's proposed amendments to the self-determination wording was presented at the Working Group on the Draft Declaration.

Indigenous peoples have also been able to use the internet and email to strategise effectively in Draft Declaration negotiations. In response to concern that states were trying to water down provisions dealing with treaties between indigenous peoples and states, indigenous peoples' representatives from around the world coordinated through conference calls and email to devise strong text on such treaties outside of the UN meetings in Geneva. As a result, when the December 2005 meeting on the Draft Declaration took place, indigenous peoples could present well-thought-out proposals on the articles dealing with treaties that had the support of a number of indigenous peoples.

Similarly, increased communication between indigenous peoples' groups has directly assisted Māori when bringing their local issues to international forums. This was seen most clearly in the degree of support provided by other indigenous peoples for Māori objections to the Foreshore and Seabed Bill and Act in UN institutions. The Pacific Indigenous Peoples' Caucus, a loosely knit group of indigenous peoples' representatives from the Pacific which is active in international forums, supported interventions by Te Rūnanga o Ngai Tahu at the UN Permanent Forum on Indigenous Issues objecting to the Foreshore and Seabed Bill in May 2004.[29] Then, in February 2005, a representative from an Australian Aboriginal organisation provided invaluable advice to me and others in arguing before the CERD Committee, on behalf of Te Rūnanga o Ngai Tahu, the Treaty Tribes Coalition and the Taranaki Māori Trust Board, that the FSA discriminates against

Māori. His assistance was invaluable because he had been part of the delegation representing Australian Aboriginal peoples in the 1999 complaint to the CERD Committee that the Australia Native Title Amendment Act 1998 discriminated against Aboriginal peoples.

Indigenous peoples' influence in world affairs

James Anaya, a leading international lawyer and academic on indigenous peoples in international law, writes: [30]

> International law especially is rooted in jurisprudential strains originating in classical Western legal thought, although today it is increasingly influenced by non-Western actors and perspectives.

One of the principal phenomena associated with globalisation, which includes the proliferation of neoliberal economic policy, is the reduction in the size and scope of the state, through both devolution of power to local entities, and transferral of power upwards to supranational bodies. Corresponding to that development is the increase in non-state institutions' ability to influence world politics. This is most obvious in the rising power of multinational corporations. Nonetheless, within this, we can see indigenous peoples increasingly playing an influential role in global affairs, especially at the UN.

Indigenous peoples have been part of a broader global push to seek greater state protection of peoples' collective rights. For example, the UN Declaration on the Rights of Indigenous Peoples expresses predominantly collective rights. Greater recognition of collective rights both adds to and complicates the earlier, almost myopic, focus on improving legal protection of individuals' rights. It broadens the emphasis of human rights to cover the needs of marginalised groups, recognising that participation in groups is a significant part of the human experience. At the same time, it creates tensions; how, for example, are conflicts between individuals' rights and collectives' rights to be resolved? In any event, indigenous peoples, alongside ethnic minorities, have been strong protagonists in galvanising global support for the recognition of less 'mainstream' cultural priorities, such as the importance of collectives.

Indigenous peoples exercise much of their political strength on the international stage through their participation at the UN, which has opened its doors to them. For example, indigenous peoples have participated actively in the UN Working Group on the Draft Declaration in a way that belies their official status as non-state actors with little formal clout in or over UN initiatives. At the same time, indigenous peoples have efficiently propelled the evolution of international human rights jurisprudence to protect their lands and self-determination, as discussed above. Most significantly, indigenous peoples have a formal role in a UN entity that ranks relatively highly in the UN institutional hierarchy. The Permanent Forum on Indigenous Issues is made up of sixteen members, of which half are chosen by indigenous peoples themselves.

Negatives of globalisation for Māori participation in the UN

Substantive difficulties: the impact of neoliberal economic agendas

The proliferation of neoliberal economic policies, which include the deregulation of multinational corporations, the commodification of resources, and so-called free trade, is frequently associated with globalisation. As stated above, globalisation is not confined to these phenomena, but they are certainly a fundamental part of it. Here, I provide some examples of how states' economic policy agendas influence, mostly negatively, the content of indigenous peoples' rights being devised within UN forums.

States' positions on the UN Declaration on the Rights of Indigenous Peoples are influenced by many factors. One is undoubtedly neoliberal economic policy. It often appears that the lens through which states analyse indigenous peoples' rights is neoliberal. The result is not always negative. It is possible that some states' comfort with the idea of increased indigenous peoples' control over their own resources is partly a result of states' willingness to devolve power to non-state entities. While devolution is a phenomenon driven by states' imperatives to increase efficiency by privatising, it may also be consistent with indigenous peoples' demands.

The economic basis for New Zealand's position on self-determination is reflected in its choice of language: it will accept a provision that allows for indigenous peoples' rights to 'self-*management*' (my emphasis). But states' neoliberal lens, while to some extent positive in this example, is inadequate from an indigenous peoples' perspective. It does not go far enough.

Indigenous peoples seek more than a devolution of power from states. More frequently, they seek recognition that there was not a legitimate transferral of power from indigenous peoples to the state in the process of colonisation. They also seek powers of self-government, rather than self-management.

In other cases, states' neoliberal agendas are quite clearly inconsistent with indigenous peoples' desire for greater protection of their traditions, as set out in the UN Declaration on the Rights of Indigenous Peoples. For example, New Zealand's approach to the cultural intellectual property rights provisions in the Draft Declaration was influenced by its desire to facilitate trade in them, which is not necessarily consistent with their protection. The 1999 New Zealand Negotiating Brief on the Draft Declaration speaks of 'legislative mechanisms to deal with the trade and export of Māori cultural property'.[31] In a similar way, states have fought strongly against indigenous peoples' land rights which might impact on private property rights. Private property is, of course, a fundamental concept in neoliberal economic theory. Further, states have been reluctant to accept provisions that recognise indigenous peoples' collective and traditional ownership of land.[32]

UN human rights treaty bodies have established jurisprudence that condones states' involvement in the conversion of indigenous peoples' traditional customary rights into modern and tradeable rights, where the indigenous peoples concerned consent. In the *Mahuika* communication, mentioned above, the UN Human Rights

Committee rejected Mahuika's argument that the replacement of Māori customary fishing rights with a commercial interest in a fishing company and fishing quota, under the Sealord Fisheries Settlement, breached his right to access culture.[33] It was particularly influenced by the extent of Māori ratification of the Sealord deal.[34] This decision represents a mixed blessing for indigenous peoples. On the one hand, positively, it recognises that indigenous peoples' rights, for example to fishing, can develop. On the other hand, possibly negatively, it reinforces the commodification of indigenous peoples' rights and modern-day trade in them, which can undermine tradition and indigenous peoples' value systems. The decision also suggests that the Human Rights Committee could be influenced by broader neoliberal economic agendas, and a perceived need for indigenous peoples to participate in them.

For many indigenous peoples, the greatest threat posed by globalisation is the proliferation of multinational corporations which exploit indigenous peoples' resources. Even casual internet searches on 'indigenous peoples, corporation and exploitation' bring up hundreds of thousands of hits.[35] Indeed, the plight of indigenous peoples from the Amazon in trying to protect their lands against exploitation from multinational corporations is well known. This problem is aggravated by states' unwillingness (and sometimes incapacity) to regulate multinational corporations, since they prioritise economic efficiency and foreign investment, which are neoliberal economic ideals. The problem for indigenous peoples who approach UN forums to seek protection of their land rights from corporate incursions is that the UN itself is unable to regulate multinational corporate behaviour effectively. States are the principal subjects of UN regulation and international law. Even though the UN has worked to devise norms to promote observances of human rights by multinational corporations, these are not binding.[36] It is for this reason, perhaps, that the UN Declaration on the Rights of Indigenous Peoples does not squarely address multinational corporate behaviour in relation to indigenous peoples, nor impose obligations on non-state entities.

Practical difficulties

Obviously, Māori face a number of practical difficulties in participating in UN forums, including a lack of financial resources and their subordinate status within the institution. The level of financial resources required to participate in global institutions in the expensive cities where the UN has its head offices, such as Geneva and New York, have proved to be prohibitive for many indigenous peoples, especially for those from developing countries. In fact, the disparity in the numbers of indigenous peoples' representatives from developed and developing countries raises the issue of whether the content of UN-derived international law on indigenous peoples' rights actually reflects the concerns of indigenous peoples from developing countries. In a similar vein, tribes within states often have varying degrees of financial capacity. This could mean that the indigenous peoples' views expressed reflect only those of the financially more powerful indigenous groups within a state. Ultimately, access to finance can therefore impact on the legitimacy of the international norms that emanate from the UN.

Moreover, indigenous peoples simply cannot compete with the resources of states when participating in the UN. This was brought home to me during the CERD Committee proceedings, when New Zealand officials arrived at the UN building in Geneva in a chauffeured car, while we had walked there after frantically photocopying our documents at the local supermarket.

Lack of funding also impacts on indigenous peoples' representatives' capacity to consult and inform their own peoples about the international forums in which indigenous peoples can participate. It is difficult to raise the necessary funds for transport and hui to hold information sessions. In turn, these information-sharing problems impact negatively on indigenous peoples' understanding of international mechanisms, and on their representatives' ability to express the views and wishes of their peoples.

Conclusion

This chapter has focused on Māori and indigenous peoples' involvement in the UN, a phenomenon related to and largely a result of globalisation. It illustrates that globalisation is both positive and negative for indigenous peoples, including Māori.

The advent of international forums where indigenous peoples can raise their agendas creates, for want of a better word, an additional battlefield. There are simply more choices in terms of venues to raise Māori issues. While the opportunities which international forums provide are unique, their very existence means that indigenous peoples are required to make strategic decisions about where best to pursue particular concerns. In cases where Māori are working collectively on a pan-Māori issue and can pool resources, such as the foreshore and seabed, the possibility of invoking both domestic and international avenues may be realistic. However, many iwi and hapū could stretch their available financial and human resources too far if, along with lobbying and seeking legal recourse domestically, they also sought to initiate international strategies.

However, on the whole, the most significant practical difficulty facing indigenous peoples participating in the UN is that it is an institution made up of states, including those that treat indigenous peoples unjustly. These very same states ultimately determine the content of UN-derived norms on indigenous peoples' rights. For example, once the Draft Declaration left the Working Group, it required endorsement by UN forums which are made up exclusively of states and in which indigenous peoples have a limited voice. Similarly, even those UN institutions that are technically independent are to some extent reliant on states' approval. Their legitimacy depends, in part, on states' willingness to comply with their reports and decisions, and members are often appointed by states.

For example, the Special Rapporteur on the Human Rights and Fundamental Freedoms of Indigenous Peoples must work with states if he or she is to effectively encourage them to comply with international human rights standards in relation to indigenous peoples. Thus, it may have been disappointing for Māori to learn that the Special Rapporteur did not produce an unqualified attack on New Zealand's treatment of Māori in New Zealand. One way or another, the same is true of UN human rights treaty bodies such as the CERD Committee. Their effectiveness is judged, at least to some extent, on states' compliance with their decisions. As a result, they are often careful to couch their censure of states in diplomatic language that is likely to receive a positive reception from states. The CERD Committee's decision on the FSA is a good example of this; the language of the decision is mild and reasonable.

Finally, the UN is a large organisation and faces its own financial difficulties. Consequently, the UN is sometimes a little unwieldy, and is often not as responsive to indigenous peoples' concerns as indigenous peoples demand. For example, the negotiations on the Draft Declaration have taken over eleven years, and the Human Rights Committee decision in the *Mahuika* proceedings, mentioned above, was delivered just short of eight years after the communication was submitted.[37]

Notes

1 The last point is made also by various others, including S. Radcliffe, N. Laurie and R. Andoline in *Indigenous Peoples and Political Transnationalism: Globalisation from Below Meets Globalisation from Above,* available at http://www.transcomm.ox.ac.uk/working%20papers/WPTC-02-05%20Radcliffe.pdf (accessed 20/12/2005).

2 United Nations Committee on the Elimination of All Forms of Racial Discrimination, 'Decision 1(66): New Zealand Foreshore and Seabed Act 2004' (11 March 2005), CERD/C/66/NZL/Dec.1.

3 American Indian Law Alliance, 'Indigenous Peoples Movement Alarmed by New Zealand's Policy' (Press Release, 9 December 2005), available at http://www.scoop.co.nz/stories/WO0512/S00209.htm (accessed 21/12/2005).

4 My involvement in UN forums includes an internship at the UN Office of the High Commissioner for Human Rights in 1998; attendance at the UN Working Group on Indigenous Populations, the UN Inter-Sessional Working Group on the Draft Declaration on the Rights of Indigenous Peoples, the UN Permanent Forum on Indigenous Issues, the UN Expert Seminar on Treaties, Agreements and Other Constructive Agreements between States and Indigenous Peoples (Geneva, December 2003), and the UN Expert Seminar on the Implementation of National Legislation and Jurisprudence Concerning Indigenous Peoples' Rights: Experiences from the Americas; facilitation of a seminar on Indigenous Peoples and International Law (Victoria University of Wellington, Wellington, 2003); and acting for Te Rūnanga o Ngai Tahu and the Treaty Tribes Coalition in the UN Committee on the Elimination of Racial Discrimination proceedings relating to the Foreshore and Seabed Act 2004.

5   S. J. Anaya, *Indigenous Peoples in International Law,* 2nd ed., New York: Oxford University Press, 2004, p. 57.

6   For an excellent introduction, see Anaya, 2004, p. 15-34.

7   Human Rights Commission Resolution 1982/19 (10 March 1982); Economic and Social Council Resolution 1982/34 (7 May 1982) UN ESCOR 1982 Supp no 1 at 26, UN Doc E/1982/82.

8   For more information on the United Nations Permanent Forum on Indigenous Issues, see United Nations website, http://www.un.org/esa/socdev/unpfii/index.html (accessed 23/12/2005).

9   Including the Special Rapporteur on Treaties, Agreements and Other Constructive Arrangements between States and Indigenous Populations, the Special Rapporteur on Indigenous Peoples and their Relationship to Land, and the Special Rapporteur on Indigenous Peoples' Permanent Sovereignty over their Natural Resources.

10 Rio Declaration on Environment and Development, UN Conference on Environment and Development, Rio de Janeiro (13 June 1999), UN Doc A/CONF.151/26(vol 1), Annex 1 (1992).

11 International Labour Organisation Convention 169 Concerning Indigenous and Tribal Peoples in Independent Countries (27 June 1989). See, for example, the arguments advanced by Te Runanga o Whare Kauri Rekohu in *Te Runanga o Whare Kauri Rekoku Inc v Attorney General* (12 October 1992) HC WN CP 682/92 Heron J, and those put forward by Apirana Mahuika in *Apirana Mahuika et al v New Zealand* Communication No 547/1993 (27 October 2000), Report of the Human Rights Committee Vol II A/56/40.

12 The states that have ratified ILO Convention 169 include: Argentina, Bolivia, Brazil, Colombia, Costa Rica, Denmark, Dominica, Ecuador, Fiji, Guatemala, Honduras, Mexico, Netherlands, Norway, Paraguay, Peru and Venezuela.

13 Convention on Biodiversity (1992) 1760 UNTS 79, article 8(j).

14 International Covenant on Civil and Political Rights (19 December 1966) 999 UNTS 171.

15 See discussion in C. Charters, 'Developments in International Law on Indigenous Peoples' Rights and their Domestic Implications', *NZULR* Vol. 21, No. 4, 2005.

16 For example, the UN Human Rights Committee has indicated that indigenous peoples have the right to self-determination by interpreting the minorities' right to culture consistently with the right to self-determination in communications brought by indigenous peoples. See *Apirana Mahuika et al v New Zealand* Communication No 547/1993 (27 October 2000) Report of the Human Rights Committee Vol II A/56/40.

17 Under, for example, the New Zealand Bill of Rights Act 1990 and the Human Rights Act 1993.

18 S. Pritchard, 'Native Title from the Perspective of International Standards' 18 *Australian Yearbook of International Law* 127, 1998, p. 128.

19 See R. Berry, 'Maori Denied Rights, UN Man Told', *New Zealand Herald,* 21 November 2005.

20 See, for example, the Human Rights Commission *Draft Discussion Document of the Human Rights Commission: Human Rights and the Treaty of Waitangi/ Te Mana i te Waitangi,* Wellington: New Zealand Human Rights Commission, 2003; and Waitangi Tribunal jurisprudence generally, available at Waitangi Tribunal, http://www.waitangi-tribunal.govt.nz/ (accessed 21/12/2005).

21 For general academic discussion of international law on self-determination, see, for example, A. Cassese, *International Law,* 2nd ed., Oxford: Oxford University Press, 2004; M. N. Shaw, *International Law,* 5th ed., Cambridge: Cambridge University Press, 2003; and I. Brownlie *Principles of Public International Law,* 6th ed., Oxford: Oxford University Press, 2003.

22 P. A. Jefferies, 'Human Rights, Foreign Policy and Religious Belief: An Asia/Pacific Perspective', *BYU Law Review* No. 885, 2000, p. 902.

23 See, in particular, articles 3 and 25 – 29 in the Draft Declaration.

24 Such as the complaint brought to the CERD Committee by Australian Aborigines against the Native Title Amendment Act 1998 and subject to CERD Committee criticism in the UN Committee on the Elimination of Racial Discrimination 'Decision 2.54 on Australia' (18 March 1999) A/54/18.

25 UN Committee on the Elimination of Racial Discrimination, 'General Recommendation XXIII: Indigenous Peoples' (18 August 1997) A/52/18, annex V, para 5. It:

calls upon States parties to recognise and protect the rights of indigenous peoples to own, develop, control and use their communal lands, territories and resources and, where they have been deprived of their lands, territories traditionally owned or otherwise inhabited or used without their free and informed consent, to take steps to return those lands and territories. Only when this is for factual reasons not possible, the right to restitution should be substituted by the right to just, fair and prompt compensation. Such compensation should as far as possible take the form of lands and territories.

26 *Mahuika*, 2000.

27 Jefferies, 2000, p. 902.

28 American Indian Law Alliance, 'Indigenous Peoples Movement Alarmed by New Zealand's Policy', Press Release, 9 December 2005, http://www.scoop.co.nz/stories/WO0512/S00209. htm (accessed 21/12/2005).

29 Indigenous Peoples' Centre for Documentation, Research and Information, 'Update 59-69' (July/October 2004); Christchurch *Press*, 'Ngai Tahu Wins Pacific Support', 14 May 2004.

30 Anaya, 2004.

31 New Zealand Negotiating Brief on the Draft Declaration on the Rights of Indigenous Peoples, Wellington: New Zealand Government, 1999.

32 See Office of the High Commissioner for Human Rights, 'Report of the Working Group Established in Accordance with Commission on Human Rights Resolution 1995/32 of 3 March 1995 on its Tenth Session', available at http://daccessdds.un.org/doc/UNDOC/GEN/ G05/157/58/PDF/G0515758.pdf?OpenElement (accessed 14/1/2006).

33 *Mahuika*, 2000.

34 Ibid.

35 Search on www.google.com on 14 January 2006.

36 See the 'Norms on the Responsibilities of Transnational Corporations and Other Business Enterprises with Regard to Human Rights', available at the United Nations High Commission for Human Rights website, http://www.unhchr.ch/huridocda/huridoca.nsf/(Symbol)/ E.CN.4.Sub.2.2003.12.Rev.2.En? Open document (accessed 14/1/2006).

37 *Mahuika*, 2000.

10

Globalisation and the Colonising State of Mind

Moana Jackson

Colonisation has a history as old as humankind. For as long as people have imagined that the grass was greener on the other side of the fence, they have embarked upon the bloody and costly business of dispossessing each other. Empires have regularly been imposed and just as regularly collapsed, and territorial borders have been rampaged across in neighbourhood raids to flaunt a new sovereignty, change a ruler, claim a bride, annex an estate, steal some treasure or simply rape and pillage. The desire to dispossess others and to take over their lives, lands and power has been a constant in world affairs.

In 1492, the dispossession took a new and especially destructive turn when the Genoese mercenary Christopher Columbus landed in the Caribbean and assumed he had found a new, faster route to the lucrative spice markets of India. His accidental stumbling into the so-called New World ushered in a distinctive and persistent period of European (and subsequently Euro-American) colonisation that has stretched way beyond the colonisers' nearest neighbours. It marked the beginnings of a haphazard but deliberately learned process of political domination and commercial exploitation that was quite specific in its intent and unlimited in its reach. Columbus may have been navigationally challenged, and he certainly had pretensions of grandeur that were never quite matched by his talents, but he initiated the long-lasting dispossession of indigenous peoples and the very first wave of globalisation.

In doing so, he also triggered what became a tipping point in the history of colonisation, because his 'discoveries' of new and distant peoples led to a profound shift in its nature, its meaning and its form. As more and more European states rushed to colonise innocent peoples who had done them no harm, they also developed a common process that privileged shared European values, institutions, laws and politics. The French and English continued to serve their own colonising interests, and the Spanish and Portuguese carried on colonising in uniquely Spanish and Portuguese ways, but they also drew upon their shared European ideas of political order, legal structure and religious certainty. Whatever continued to make them different from (and suspicious of) each other, and the forces that drove them still regularly to go to war, became relative when measured against the greater difference they would collectively see in indigenous peoples.

A transnational bond and a unity of intent developed over the time that encouraged an intangible feeling of European commonality, rather like that of a family that stands together against the world while continuing to fight among its own members. Thus many years later in 1664, when the English took the lands that the Netherlands had earlier seized from the Haudenosaunee and substituted New York for New Amsterdam, they introduced a change of colonising style but continued to act according to values that had been forged through centuries of shared religious, social and political tradition. The battles they had fought with each other could not obscure the fact that they were also parties to ongoing alliances, which just over twenty years later would see the English ask a Dutch nobleman, William of Orange, to be their king. Being a colonising state often involved taking advantage of one's European brothers and sisters, but it never meant entirely forsaking them, because in contrast to indigenous peoples they were all simply the best. Within a century of Columbus's first landfall, colonisation was becoming a European-based culture with its own distinct practices, ideologies, justifications, myths and lifestyle.

On the shores of the island that its people called Guanahani, Columbus acted out and established some of the ideas that would become fundamental to the culture as a global phenomenon (and its associated and distinctively novel form of state-sanctioned terrorism). In actions that some say were merely the products of his time, but which set precedents for centuries ahead, he first of all placed a flag in the sand and claimed the land in the name of his sponsoring Spanish monarchs and his god. Although the local Taino and Lucayan people had their own views of legitimate authority and how it had to be acquired, he assumed a superior right to be their sovereign. Like every coloniser before and after him, he made a statement of political power and purported to assert a constitutional legitimacy, because dispossession always begins with a will to rule. Whether the intention is a lightning hit-and-run raid, a pre-emptive attack to preserve 'vital national interest', or a longer-term desire to hit and stay in someone else's land, the papa or the base of colonisation's admittedly strange whakapapa is always the assertion and retrenchment of power. When Columbus performed his odd ritual of flag waving, he therefore assumed that it transferred the pre-existing Taino authority to him, and thus set in train the acts of annexation that would be followed by every other coloniser from Francisco Pizzaro to James Cook and William Hobson.

Over the next few days and on all of his return voyages, Columbus also plundered what resources he could, including the bodies of the 'timorous if savage natives' as slaves. He was unable to find the spices he promised or the gold he hungered for, but he assumed a right to exploit whatever he saw. Land and people that were there to be annexed were also commodities to be taken. That had always been the colonising case, but he expanded the possibilities and the legal excuses, so that when millions of the poor and oppressed subsequently left Europe to improve their lot in America or Aotearoa, they assumed that they had the right to do so at the expense of indigenous peoples. Learning how and why that was so, and accepting the myths of civilised progress or racial superiority that rationalised their intent, became part of the process that transformed colonisation from a raid to a culture. The culture itself would never be just an economic exercise, because dispossession is much more complex than that, and cultures always exist beyond the individual motives of those who learn and live within them; but the quest for profit certainly drove the colonisers to what they thought was the better life.

Another power that Columbus claimed on Guanahani was exercised as the people followed their own customs and welcomed him with gifts. His response was to act as if they thought he was a god and revered him because he 'came from heaven', which was a mark of his own egotism and, more importantly, an assumption that he had the power to read other people's minds and define what they thought or should think. When many of them subsequently protested at some of his actions, he killed them, which was the most sovereign divinely wrathful right of all. In the following centuries, the deaths of indigenous peoples were to become colonisation's constant companion, and changing the minds of those who were left to live was their most crucial purpose. For cultures are a site of learning about how to view the world, and the evolution of a colonising culture was also a colonising way that indigenous peoples were meant to think.

The rituals Columbus performed and the massacres he countenanced are a long time ago now, but they continue to influence the course of international politics and law as well as the shifting currents of trade and economics. Indeed, the rapid expansion of globalisation that seems to have come out of nowhere in the last three decades is actually the product of the history that began with his little flag waving and his assumption of a right to take. Its ideologies and practices require the same assertions of power in the pursuit of political and economic dominance, and the same unswerving confidence that a will to dispossess can be manufactured into a right. And it certainly sustains the demand that one way of thinking can be a universal truth that should be accepted by all.

The indigenous relations of the Taino and Lucayan still struggle with the state of mind and the affairs of state that were initiated on

Guanahani. There are no direct descendants, because everyone on the island was killed or died of introduced diseases within twenty years of Columbus's landfall. But the legacy remained.

In the early contacts our people had with Pākehā, we were quick to see the advantages in some of the new technologies and commercial opportunities, just as we were intrigued by the different religion they brought and the new skill of writing they carried in their books. But adaptation is never the same as acquiescence to the power that brings the new. As long as we were secure in the political power of rangatiratanga and retained authority over the resource base, we controlled both the practice and the ideologies of economic change. Accumulating new sources of wealth in an expanding market served and enhanced our power and enabled us to resist the colonising Crown claims of absolute sovereignty over us. Cook waving a flag in Mercury Bay and Hobson waving one to reaffirm his claim that in the Treaty of Waitangi, we had ceded our authority, could be tolerated with confident bemusement because we knew in our own law and history that to do so would have been culturally incomprehensible and constitutionally impossible.

But the culture of colonisation has never had any place for contesting views of power, and in a long and now familiar history, we were subjected to the same kind of totalising dispossession as the Taino and other indigenous peoples. It may have differences in kind, but oppression is always oppression, and the myths that justified it have rarely varied, whether they were made up by the Belgians in the Congo or the English here. Our power was subsumed into theirs. Our resources, both economic and cultural, were confiscated or marginalised, and our once proudly expressed self-determination became a selflessly desperate struggle to survive. We became the subjects of the colonisers and the servants of their economy.

As we now endeavour to recover and seek redress for our dispossession, we are caught up in the most recent fervour of globalisation. Since the 1980s, it has shaped the government response to our grievances and defined how many people now think about our rights and our status. It has been the context within which the Treaty of Waitangi has been reconfigured as a testing ground for property rights, rather than the constitutional and political text that all treaties are, and it has attempted to squeeze our innate status as tangata whenua to fit within the global interests of consumerism, or the need to be players in the market. In a twist on the ancient colonising myth, the economic development we might want is being confused with the complete self-determination we are entitled to.

Among the many vicissitudes that globalisation brings and the challenges it poses, it is that confusion which is perhaps the most problematic. It equates growing the asset base with the idea of kaitiakitanga, without recognising the difference between the skill to improve economic indicators, and the power to protect the base and determine what that means. It assumes that the free market will free us from welfare dependency, without acknowledging that it was the playing of the market by others that took our independence away. It fails to acknowledge that without a new reclaiming of the political authority we once had, we remain the servants of the economy rather than the authors of its course and its benefits. The jargon of globalised inevitability, the argument that there is no alternative or no other 'reality', has become the seductive story that influences and changes our thinking about who we are and what we might become. In the genuine desire to improve the lot of our people, we lose sight of the fact that the New Right is the old righteousness of a colonising order.

Our people have always believed that there is never just one truth or one way of doing things. The very notion of our whakapapa implies generations of different stories layered on top of one another. Telling stories was always a journey to the point of enlightenment that we knew as the explanation or the whakamārama. Part of the challenge in reconfiguring the current imbalance and reclaiming the proper exercise of our self determination is to know the globalising whakapapa and the messages it conveys about rights, what reality is, and even the way we should think about the world. The whakapapa resides partly in the esoteric debates and dismal science of economics and the equally dismal, if frightening, rhetoric of the New Age colonisers, who still justify invading other countries as pre-emptive strikes or equate their 'national interests' with a right to intervene anywhere in the world. But it can also be found in much more mundane circumstances. It is in our own stories of what may be called the little everyday colonisations that we might most profitably find explanations, and a means of full and final redress. For in our own stories, there has always been a certain power and a reassurance that waving a flag on a beach and asserting that a desire for plunder is the only path to improvement are, in the end, only a storytelling too.

A shopping mall story

Whakapapa is like a history of repetitious beginnings. Each new event, each generation of ideas and actions that shape human lives is a product of those that have gone before. Nothing exists in isolation or arises spontaneously in a vacuum of immaculate conception. Instead, the present and future are only the past revisited – ka puta mai – things come into being, are born of something else.

When Māori people speak of the past as i ngā rā o mua, we know it is the days before and that we carry them with us, rather like walking back to the future with history dogging our footsteps. That understanding is not quite the same as the wisdom in the old adage that the more things change, the more they stay the same, because history is naturally an evolution of sorts. However, there is a prescience in history and the present, a sense that comprehending what Patricia Grace has called the 'now-time' means seeking out the symmetries and similarities with the past.

In the current and often confusing world times of globalisation and neoliberal market ideologies, where capital flows across borders as it has never done before, and multinational companies have bigger budgets than many states have ever had, it is easy to think that it is indeed part of a new world order. Its apparent newness then makes its problems seem insoluble and its inequities seem intractable. However, Māori and other indigenous peoples are increasingly aware that its beginnings and purpose are much the same as those which were advocated by people who first profited from the colonisation of slavery and the slavery of slavery. Behind the determined ideologies of its advocates are some sadly familiar stories where the links between the past and present can be found in the simplest of places and times.

A new mall has just been built in Lower Hutt.[1] It is not a big mall by world standards, although it probably surpasses most others in the ugliness of its external architecture. Inside, it has the same shiny appearance of others and many of the same shops one could find in Auckland or Oakland. In a sense, it is part of a mall culture, of which the biggest and brightest is the West Edmonton Mall in Canada. It is featured in the Guinness Book of Records as the biggest shopping complex in the world, and has over eight hundred shops that are constructed around theme parks, an ice-skating palace, an indoor water world and imitation oceans with marooned pirate ships. In many ways, it represents the vanities of the 1990s building boom, with its homage to a besotted shop-till-you-drop mentality and the credo that greed is good.

Yet rather like the old statues that honour colonial heroes in marble or stone devoid of context, it is also an unremarked symbol of the imperatives that have characterised the colonisation of the world's indigenous peoples. It represents the same glitzy me-first consumerism that was one of the prime motivations which sent millions of people from Europe to dispossess whole nations who had never done them any harm. It offers the promise of a 'better life' in the accumulation of goods, in much the same way as the original colonisers sought to improve their lot by taking the goods, the power and the lives of indigenous peoples.

The symbolism and the symmetries are rendered more acute by the presence in the West Edmonton Mall of a large retail outlet called 'The Bay'. Situated just down the shopping aisle from the Galaxyland amusement park, The Bay proudly promotes itself as Canada's oldest department store. Some of its décor is a reproduction of pioneering rusticity, and its brochures feature images of old fur trappers standing outside snow-covered log cabins in what seems a homage to a proud history. However, an untold part of its real history can be found only across town, in an old military base. Fort Edmonton was one of the original army redoubts built by the colonisers as they moved west across Canada and took the land from the First Nations peoples. The fort was partly funded and the surrounding area mapped by officials of the Hudson Bay Company, the parent of the current department store.

The origins of The Bay, therefore, do not lie in harmlessly quaint images of log cabin simplicity, but in a more dubious merger between the seventeenth century European fascination with exclusive goods such as furs and gold, and the move by many colonising governments to bring profit and dispossession together within a company structure. Under its establishment charter granted by King Charles II to 'seek out commerce and opportunities' for the Crown, the Hudson Bay Company built its first local trading post in the fort and exercised the administrative powers it had been given to establish a monopoly over the fur trade, and exert authority over 'all lands whose rivers and streams drain into the Hudson Bay'. It assumed all of the power and property that the colonisers of Europe believed were their prerogatives. Its 'factor', or CEO, became a de facto governor, and its trade dealings with the local indigenous peoples easily crossed the line from the profit seeking of business to the politics of assuming power.

Canada's 'first department store' was actually its first transnational colonising corporate, a sort of prototype state-owned enterprise in which the bottom line of trading interests was also the invisible hand of the colonising will to rule. It was a mechanism to plunder and profit, but it was also contextualised within the right that Europe had assumed to dispossess indigenous peoples. Like the English or Dutch East Indies Companies and the French or Danish West Indies Trading Corporations (and even Edward Gibbon Wakefield's New Zealand Company), it saw indigenous lands as the sites of potential sovereignty and a new global marketplace where European power could be established and resources taken. Indeed, as the fairly typical charter of the joint venture Virginia Company stated, their aims were to trade or access such wealth as was available, while implementing so 'noble a work' as the conversion of the heathens and the establishment of a governing council. Any free market was to be freely controlled in their interests, and as political alliances changed in Europe and new economic ideologies became faddish, those interests remained paramount.

When Britain became the most successful coloniser and controlled most of the world's navigation routes, it attempted to close the market down with restrictive regulations about the movement of goods and the imposition of high tariffs. The market was only as free as England's mercantilists wanted it to be, although the indigenous peoples whose lands and bodies were its main source of raw materials were singularly unfree.

By the time the New Zealand Company was established, England's monopoly on colonisation was so complete that it could permit a lowering of tariffs and regulations. Trade entered a laissez-faire or relatively free stage, underpinned by economic theories that not only stressed the need to let the invisible hand of the market roam free, but also assumed that free trade and individual property rights were the key ingredients of civilisation and democracy. Taking indigenous resources to Europe or trading with the Europeans who had decided to stay in indigenous lands became a route to wealth and the mythical route to human progress. The investors in the New Zealand Company did not share in the new-found freedom, because the Crown itself chose to directly implement its credo of buying land cheaply from the 'natives' and selling it at a profit to the colonisers. As the wars and other colonising tools exacted our dispossession, the market in our resources became increasingly free to the colonisers, subject only to Crown rules and the openness of the 'home' market in England. Our previous entrepreneurial spirit was denied as the land base was taken and our power to determine its form and extent was diminished. Market forces were controlled by the very visible hand of someone else.

The arguments that the colonisers used to justify their entry and the mechanisms they used to control the market under the guise of a mutually beneficial free trade are remarkably similar to those used in the last twenty years by the advocates of globalisation. They imposed a way of thinking about the purpose of economics and the commodification of things that had once been treasures, and they promised development and civilisation as our salvation, even as they took away or redefined the means by which we could benefit and define what that meant.

Today, the assumption that colonisation was more of a shonky property transaction than a denial of power has led to the return of some resources to Māori, along with the mantra that it is the path out of grievance mode. Old ideologies are revisited, and we are encouraged to return to the market and be entrepreneurs again, without the independent authority that once made that possible. We achieve some commercial success, but the disparities between our wealth and that of Pākehā are now exacerbated by a divisive corporate elitism that separates many of our people from each other. Our poor and unwell retreat into a poverty where asking questions about what is happening just seems too hard, and those who have become rich often see no need to ask at all.

In that context, the symmetries between the mall as a symbol of the supposed new world order and the old colonising corporations seem especially clear. The malls are often chartered to return profits to somewhere else, and the only role they expect of local communities is to buy or produce at the cheap rates they demand. In their seductive surface glamour, they promise an innocent excitement, but offer only a homogenisation of values where changing fashion has become the new definition of choice, and designer labels and logos are the substitute for meaningful difference. They seek to change reality as colonisers have always done, and the ideologies they foster and the power they wield are part of the history of colonisation reproducing itself in the present.

A story of singing animals and talking grass

Colonisation has always been a complex process. The assumptions it has made and the way it has taken power from indigenous peoples have varied over time and circumstance. The idea that power comes from the barrel of a gun has been a handy colonising truism, and every act of dispossession has, at some stage, required the colonisers to wage wars, commit horrendous massacres and perpetrate an often unrelenting physical violence. However, power can also be exercised in less overtly violent ways, through attacks on the souls and minds of people to be dispossessed. Destroying the world-view and culture of indigenous peoples has always been as important as taking their lives, because the actual process of disempowerment, the key purpose of any colonisation, has to function at the spiritual and psychic level as well as the physical and political.

The ideologies behind the corporate interests of the sparkling malls represent one variant of dispossession that does not appear to be overtly violent but that is, nevertheless, sourced in ancient precedents about commodification and the primacy of property which have been crucial in the design of colonisation. In their multinational reach, the mall corporations are often intimately connected with the exploitation of other people in sweat shops and the despoliation of their natural resources, but they also symbolise the exercise of a different power that may be called the power to define. When people assume that they have the right and ability to define what is worthy and 'real' and then impose that upon someone else, while distorting or dismissing any contesting views, they are colonising at an especially primal level. In the context of the mall, they are trying to change people's minds by confusing the market value of something with the values that a different culture might hold about it.

A similar process is at work in the globalising of bioethics and the issue of genetic modification. The debate that has recently surrounded the issue has been frustrating and confusing for Māori, because it has raised profound and deeply philosophical questions about how we define ourselves, what value we place upon whakapapa and the ira tangata, and how we might balance the integrity of our identity with the wish for good health and well-being. Those sorts of questions have always been dismissed or redefined by the colonisers when we have asked them, and they continue to be misrepresented as little more than a vaguely spiritual and quaint subtext.

Consultation on the issue has merely led to a feeling that the Māori 'perspective' that was being sought was only a 'cultural' explanation of something in which 'normality' and 'truth' had already been determined. The response is usually framed in the name of scientific rationality or economic reality, but is actually just another example of the power to define. It establishes what the definer thinks of as the only truth, and then reads our minds in order to redefine and diminish the worth of what we have to say by reducing our complex cosmogonies and intellectual traditions to something that is lesser. It diminishes and denies the fact that every indigenous nation, Māori included, have always had systems of knowledge and understanding, law and government, values and value. In effect, it denies the validity of other ways of seeing the world, and thus privileges its own gaze above all others.

The confidence to dismiss or demean Māori perceptions has been determined by a set of social and cultural assumptions that were learned as part of the culture and dialectic of colonisation. It indicates a stubbornly held certainty about the nature and history of the Western scientific method, and an unwillingness to accept that, like every other way of researching, testing and analysing facts or assertions, it is culture bound. Like the English common law, which claims an inherent impartiality of almost God-like perfection, or the idea that the economy is driven by immutable and mysterious market 'forces', it was thought into being and has merely taken upon itself its own kind of divine perfection.

The power to define remains at the core of the new globalisation. It is exercised not only in the definitive extolling of genetic modification, but in every context where Māori perspectives are made subordinate. When the (now failed) Scottish company PPL Pharmaceuticals attempted to insert human genes into sheep on the lands of Ngai Te Rangi in the mid 1990s, the power was exposed with the clarity of spot-lit mannequins in a mall display. Like the issues that had earlier been forecast in the Wai 262 claim to the Waitangi Tribunal on the protection of our knowledge and our flora and fauna, it raised serious issues of control, protection and the right and power to define our own world.

At the first hui held in Tauranga to consider the PPL experiments, many of the young people present admitted their confusion about the project and the questions it raised. However, they were at least clear that something seemed not quite right, as if ancient fires were being lit and puzzling questions were being asked about, 'Why do we need to know this?' One young man summed up this sense with the comment that he didn't want to hear sheep singing waiata on his way to work, while another wondered whether human genes might also be inserted into plants so that the grass would talk as well. Their comments were greeted with quiet laughter, but also a general awareness that in many areas of Pākehā society, the ethics of the issue were being raised after the work had started, and that the sorts of questions which would have been asked within a Māori intellectual framework about the rightness of mixing any genes and its impact on the totality of whakapapa were not being considered.

Instead, genetic modification was simply accepted as an unchallengeable given, and risk was being debated as something to be managed after the fact, rather than predicted with forethought as an essential step in deciding whether the particular line of enquiry should even have been contemplated. The technological feasibility of inserting human genes in another species was accepted as the starting point of the discourse, rather than the more fundamental querying of whether feasibility necessarily equated with wisdom. Western science had in fact set the parameters of the research, as well as the meaning of the discourse that rationalised it.

Much has changed since the early 1990s, but the basic non-Māori approach remains the same, and bioethics has become a new and contradictory designer label that seeks to rationalise genetic modification experimentation purely on the basis of 'reality' and a supposedly superior intellectual framework. There is now even a hierarchy of genetic acceptability, in which human genes are regarded as worthy of special consideration or regulation because they are somehow more valuable than those of other species. The genes of 'man' have assumed dominion in a New Age dualism that sets them apart from all others. Even the oft repeated question and reply, 'He aha te mea nui? He tangata, he tangata' has been redefined in a Biblical notion of human primacy, instead of being read as part of a whakapapa of interrelationships with the earth mother.

In such a construct, ethics and moral restraint are narrowly defined concepts that seem to be too easily swayed by the hope of economic reward or the promise of medical breakthrough. The latter is understandable, especially for those suffering from diseases that currently seem incurable, but there are broader and more difficult questions that are not being addressed about whether in fact a cure, or the process of finding a cure, might create something more problematic than the original illness in social, human, spiritual and environmental terms. The issues are complex. Silencing or reconceptualising Māori questions does not make them any more amenable to resolution. Instead, it merely maintains another example of the colonising power to define in the changing context of a new but old globalisation.

The lessons in the stories

There are threads of understanding that can be found in every story if the teller controls the telling and the meaning. In the globalised reality that was spawned on the beach on Guanahani, the stories told by the colonisers have collapsed into misleading myths and deceptive, if beguiling, lies. Although untrue and often provably wrong, they continue to set empirical events underway and create a reality where there does often seem to be no alternative. But realities are always made, and the challenge that has faced Indigenous Peoples since 1492 is how to re-establish other views of the world that are less damaging and more hopeful.

The disjunction between economics and self-determination, or between the contesting moralities of genetic modification, is caused by many layers of ideas, practices and assumptions of power, because the patterns of cultures are always multi-faceted. They have threatened and in some cases destroyed much of what is good and unique in being Māori in their insistence that we must constantly 'get real', and work within and attach our 'perspectives' to the world they define. However, Māori and many others continue to learn from the lessons of history, and more of our people now struggle to critique and understand that the new model of economic development espoused in globalisation merely empowers the old colonising state and the forces that established it. We have also learned that just as the apparent gospel truth of laissez-faire economics gave way to mercantilist interests before they swung back again, so the current questions about and failures of the present global system make it increasingly vulnerable. There is no easy path to deconstruct globalisation, to de-colonise the current forms of inequity and inequality, and there is an awful truth in Frederick Douglass's reminder that power never gives up of itself without a struggle.[2] It never has, and it never will, but knowing something of its whakapapa and finding power in our own stories and the alternatives they might offer to change constitutions, economics and the ethics of life still offer hope for a better and more substantive enlightenment.

Notes

1 Lower Hutt is a suburb of Wellington.
2 F. Douglass, 'West India Emancipation: Speech delivered at Canandaigua, New York, August 4, 1857' in P. S. Foner (ed) *The Life and Writings of Frederick Douglass,* Vol. 2, New York: International Publishers, 1950, p. 437.

Appendix[1]

The Māori Version

Te Tiriti o Waitangi

Ko Wikitoria te Kuini o Ingarangi i tana mahara atawai ki nga Rangatira me nga Hapu o Nu Tirani i tana hiahia hoki kia tohungia ki a ratou o ratou rangatiratanga me to ratou wenua, a kia mau tonu hoki te Rongo ki a ratou me te Atanoho hoki kua whakaaro ia he mea tika kia tukua mai tetahi Rangatira – hei kai wakarite ki nga Tangata Maori o Nu Tirani – kia whakaaetia e nga Rangatira Maori te Kawanatanga o te Kuini ki nga wahikatoa o te Wenua nei me nga Motu – na te mea hoki he tokomaha ke nga tangata o tona Iwi Kua noho ki tenei wenua, a e haere mai nei.

Na ko te Kuini e hiahia ana kia wakaritea te Kawanatanga kia kaua ai nga kino e puta mai ki te tangata Maori ki te Pakeha e noho ture kore ana.

Na, kua pai te Kuini kia tukua a hau a Wiremu Hopihona he Kapitana i te Roiara Nawi hei Kawana mo nga wahi katoa o Nu Tirani e tukua aianei, amua atu ki te Kuini, e mea atu ana ia ki nga Rangatira o te wakaminenga o nga hapu o Nu Tirani me era Rangatira atu enei ture ka korerotia nei.

Ko Te Tuatahi
Ko nga Rangatira o te wakaminenga me nga Rangatira katoa hoki ki hai i uru ki taua wakaminenga ka tuku rawa atu ki te Kuini o Ingarani ake tonu atu - te Kawanatanga katoa o o ratou wenua.

Ko Te Tuarua

Ko te Kuini o Ingarani ka wakarite ka wakaae ki nga Rangatira ki nga hapu – ki nga tangata katoa o Nu Tirani te tino rangatiratanga o o ratou wenua o ratou kainga me o ratou taonga katoa. Otiia ko nga Rangatira o te wakaminenga me nga Rangatira katoa atu ka tuku ki te Kuini te hokonga o era wahi wenua e pai ai te tangata nona te Wenua – ki te ritenga o te utu e wakaritea ai e ratou ko te kai hoko e meatia nei e te Kuini hei kai hoko mona.

Ko Te Tuatoru

Hei wakaritenga mai hoki tenei mo te wakaaetanga ki te Kawanatanga o te Kuini – Ka tiakina e te Kuini o Ingarani nga tangata Maori katoa o Nu Tirani ka tukua ki a ratou nga tikanga katoa rite tahi ki ana mea ki nga tangata o Ingarani.

[signed] William Hobson Consul & Lieutenant Governor

Na ko matou ko nga Rangatira o te Wakaminenga o nga hapu o Nu Tirani ka huihui nei ki Waitangi ko matou hoki ko nga Rangatira o Nu Tirani ka kite nei i te ritenga o enei kupu, ka tangohia ka wakaaetia katoatia e matou, koia ka tohungia ai o matou ingoa o matou tohu.

Ka meatia tenei ki Waitangi i te ono o nga ra o Pepueri i te tau kotahi mano, e waru rau e wa te kau o to tatou Ariki.

The English translation of the Maori version[2]

The Treaty of Waitangi

Victoria, the Queen of England, in her concern to protect the chiefs and the sub-tribes of New Zealand and in her desire to preserve their chieftainship[3] and their lands to them and to maintain peace[4] and good order considers it just to appoint an administrator[5] one who will negotiate with the people of New Zealand to the end that their chiefs will agree to the Queen's Government being established over all parts of this land and (adjoining) islands[6] and also because there are many of her subjects already living on this land and others yet to come. So the Queen desires to establish a government so that no evil will come to Maori and European living in a state of lawlessness. So the Queen has appointed me, William Hobson a Captain in the Royal Navy to be Governor for all parts of New Zealand (both those) shortly to be received by the Queen and (those) to be received hereafter and presents[7] to the chiefs of the Confederation chiefs of the subtribes of New Zealand and other chiefs these laws set out here.

The First
The Chiefs of the Confederation and all the chiefs who have not joined that Confederation give absolutely to the Queen of England for ever the complete government[8] over their land.

The Second
The Queen of England agrees to protect the chiefs, the subtribes and all the people of New Zealand in the unqualified exercise[9] of their chieftainship over their lands, villages and all their treasures[10]. But on the other hand the Chiefs of the Confederation and all the Chiefs will sell[11] land to the Queen at a price agreed to by the person owning it and by the person buying it (the latter being) appointed by the Queen as her purchase agent.

The Third
For this agreed arrangement therefore concerning the Government of the Queen, the Queen of England will protect all the ordinary people of New Zealand and will give them the same rights and duties[12] of citizenship as the people of England.[13]

[Signed] William Hobson Consul & Lieutenant-Governor

So we, the Chiefs of the Confederation of the subtribes of New Zealand meeting here at Waitangi having seen the shape of these words which we accept and agree to record our names and our marks thus.

Was done at Waitangi on the sixth of February in the year of our Lord 1840.

The English version

The Treaty of Waitangi

Her Majesty Victoria Queen of the United Kingdom of Great Britain and Ireland regarding with Her Royal Favour the Native Chiefs and Tribes of New Zealand and anxious to protect their just Rights and Property and to secure to them the enjoyment of Peace and Good Order has deemed it necessary in consequence of the great number of Her Majesty's Subjects who have already settled in New Zealand and the rapid extension of Emigration both from Europe and Australia which is still in progress to constitute and appoint a functionary properly authorized to treat with the Aborigines of New Zealand for the recognition of Her Majesty's Sovereign authority over the whole or any part of those islands.

Her Majesty therefore being desirous to establish a settled form of Civil Government with a view to avert the evil consequences which must result from the absence of the necessary Laws and Institutions alike to the native population and to Her subjects has been graciously pleased to empower and to authorize 'me William Hobson a Captain' in Her Majesty's Royal Navy Consul and Lieutenant Governor of such parts of New Zealand as may be or hereafter shall be ceded to Her Majesty to invite the confederated and independent Chiefs of New Zealand to concur in the following Articles and Conditions.

Article the First
The Chiefs of the Confederation of the United Tribes of New Zealand and the separate and independent Chiefs who have not become members of the Confederation cede to Her Majesty the Queen of England absolutely and without reservation all the rights and powers of Sovereignty which the said Confederation

or Individual Chiefs respectively exercise or possess, or may be supposed to exercise or to possess, over their respective Territories as the sole Sovereigns thereof.

Article the Second
Her Majesty the Queen of England confirms and guarantees to the Chiefs and Tribes of New Zealand and to the respective families and individuals thereof the full exclusive and undisturbed possession of their Lands and Estates Forests Fisheries and other properties which they may collectively or individually possess so long as it is their wish and desire to retain the same in their possession; but the Chiefs of the United Tribes and the individual Chiefs yield to Her Majesty the exclusive right of Preemption over such lands as the proprietors thereof may be disposed to alienate at such prices as may be agreed upon between the respective Proprietors and persons appointed by Her Majesty to treat with them in that behalf.

Article the Third
In consideration thereof Her Majesty the Queen of England extends to the Natives of New Zealand Her royal protection and imparts to them all the Rights and Privileges of British Subjects.

[Signed] W Hobson Lieutenant Governor

Now therefore We the Chiefs of the Confederation of the United Tribes of New Zealand being assembled in Congress at Victoria in Waitangi and We the Separate and Independent Chiefs of New Zealand claiming authority over the Tribes and Territories which are specified after our respective names, having been made fully to understand the Provisions of the foregoing Treaty, accept and enter into the same in the full spirit and meaning thereof in witness of which we have attached our signatures or marks at the places and the dates respectively specified.

Done at Waitangi this Sixth day of February in the year of Our Lord one thousand eight hundred and forty.

Notes

1   This Appendix is based on the translation and notes outlined in I. H.Kawharu (ed.), *Waitangi: Maori and Pakeha Perspectives of the Treaty of Waitangi*, Auckland: Oxford University Press, 1989.

2   An attempt at a reconstruction of the literal translation.

3   'Chieftainship': this concept has to be understood in the context of Maori social and political organisation as at 1840. The accepted approximation today is 'trusteeship'; see New Zealand Maori Council Kaupapa 1983.

4   'Rongo': 'Peace', seemingly a missionary usage (rongo - to hear, i.e. hear the 'Word' - the 'message' of peace and goodwill, etc).

5   'Chief' ('Rangatira') here is of course ambiguous. Clearly a European could not be a Maori, but the word could well have implied a trustee-like role, rather than that of a mere 'functionary'. Maori speeches at Waitangi in 1840 refer to Hobson being or becoming a 'father' for the Maori people. Certainly this attitude has been held towards the person of the Crown down to the present day - hence the continued expectations and commitments entailed in the Treaty.

6   'Islands', i.e. neighbouring, not of the Pacific.

7   'Making', i.e. 'offering' or *'saying'* - but *not* 'inviting to concur' (cf English version).

8   'Government': 'kawanatanga'. There could be no possibility of the Maori signatories having any understanding of government in the sense of 'sovereignty' i.e. any understanding on the basis of experience or cultural precedent.

9   'Unqualified exercise' of the chieftainship: this would emphasise to a chief the Queen's intention to give them complete control according to *their* customs. 'Tino' has the connotation of 'quintessential'.

10   'Treasures': 'taonga'. As submissions to the Waitangi Tribunal concerning the Maori language have made clear, 'taonga' refers to all dimensions of a tribal group's estate, material and non-material – heirlooms and wahi tapu (sacred places), ancestral lore and whakapapa (genealogies), etc.

11   'Sale and purchase': 'hokonga'. Hoko means to buy or sell.

12   'Rights and duties': Maori 'tikanga'. While tika means right, correct, (e.g. 'e tika hoki' means 'that is right'), 'tikanga' most commonly refers to custom(s), for example of the marae (ritual forum); and custom(s) clearly includes the notion of duty and obligation.

13   There is, however, a more profound problem about 'tikanga'. There is a real sense here of the Queen 'protecting' (i.e. allowing the preservation of) the *Maori* people's tikanga (i.e. customs), since no Maori could have had any understanding whatever of *British* tikanga (i.e. rights and duties of British subjects). This, then, reinforces the guarantees in Article 2.

Notes on Contributors

Maria Bargh
Ngāti Kea, Ngāti Tuarā of Te Arawa and Ngāti Awa. She has a PhD in Political Science and International Relations from the Australian National University. She is currently a lecturer in Māori Studies at Victoria University of Wellington.

Claire Charters
Ngāti Whakaue, is a senior lecturer in law at Victoria University of Wellington, although currently on leave to complete a PhD at the University of Cambridge in the UK. She teaches and publishes in comparative and international indigenous peoples rights and has acted for a number of iwi both domestically and internationally.

Moana Jackson
Ngāti Kahungunu, Ngāti Porou. Internationally recognised indigenous rights lawyer, writer and researcher and was instrumental in establishing the Māori Legal Service and the Māori Law Commission. He also lectures in the Māori Laws and Philosophy programme at Te Wānanga o Raukawa.

Bridget Robson
Ngāti Raukawa, is a Māori health researcher with Te Rōpū Rangahau Hauora a Eru Pōmare, the Eru Pōmare Māori Health Research Centre at the Wellington School of Medicine and Health Sciences, University of Otago.

Cherryl Waerea-i-te-rangi Smith
Of Ngāti Apa, Kahungunu and Te Aitanga a Hauiti. She is the Co-Director of Te Atawhai O Te Ao: Independent Māori Institute for Environment and Health in Whanganui. She has a PhD from the University of Auckland and is a grandmother. She has been writing and talking about globalisation, the Treaty and impacts on Māori for the last 12 years.

Maui Solomon
Moriori, Kai Tahu, Pākehā. Maui is a Wellington Barrister who has specialised in representing Moriori and Māori tribes in a range of Treaty-related issues over the past 20 years including fisheries, Māori land, Treaty claims and settlements, cultural and intellectual property rights and research and development initiatives. He has also been involved in international advocacy for the rights of indigenous peoples for the past 16 years and is currently president-elect of the International Society of Ethnobiologists, an organisation dedicated to working in a collaborative partnership between scientists, indigenous peoples and researchers on issues related to traditional knowledge and intellectual property rights issues.

Annette Sykes
Ngāti Pikiao, Ngāti Makino, Te Arawa. Lawyer and activist based in Rotorua.

Alice Te Punga Somerville
Te Atiawa ki Waiwhetu. She has a PhD in English Literature and American Indian Studies from Cornell University and is a Lecturer in the School of English, Theatre, Film and Media Studies, Victoria University of Wellington, where she teaches Māori, Pacific and Indigenous writing in English. She is currently working on a book project, *Once Were Pacific*, which explores articulation of Māori connection with the Pacific, and also writes the occasional poem.

Teanau Tuiono
Ngai Takoto, Ngapuhi, Atiu, Parent, Activist, IT Specialist.

Glossary

Hapū	a subtribe or family group within an iwi
Hauora	health and well-being
He aha te mea nui?	
He tangata, he tangata	What is the most important thing? It is people
Hui	a meeting or conference especially for discussion of Māori matters
I ngā rā o mua	in the days before
Ira tangata	line of descendants
Iwi	a Māori tribe
Ka puta mai	to come into being, to be born
Kaitiaki	traditional guardians
Kaitiakitanga	guardianship or stewardship
Karakia	prayer, invocations
Kaumātua	elder
Kaupapa	a principle or policy or strategy; an agenda or objective
Kawa	the etiquette observed on a marae
Kāwanatanga	governance
Kei te pai	it is alright
Kohanga reo	Māori language pre-school
Kōrero	talk, discussion, a meeting for this
Kura	school
Kura Kaupapa Māori	Māori immersion school
Manaakitanga	taking care of each other
Marae	meeting house, also encompasses the courtyard, meeting house and dining hall
Mātauranga	knowledge
Mātauranga Māori	Māori traditional knowledge
Mauri	life force
Moana	ocean

Moko	facial markings
Mokomokai	shrunken heads
Pākehā	non-Māori New Zealander usually of European descent
Papa-tū-ā-nuku	the Earth Mother
Rangatahi	young people
Rangatiratanga	chieftainship, sovereignty
Raupatu	confiscation
Rohe	region, tribal district
Rongoā	medicine
Rūnanga	an assembly or council
Taonga	tangible and intangible treasures
Tangata whenua	Māori people of a particular locality, Māori people generally especially in their capacity as indigenous people of New Zealand
Tapu	sacredness
Te Moana Nui ā Kiwa	Pacific Ocean
Tikanga	customs, protocol
Tino rangatiratanga	full (Māori) sovereignty, self-determination
Tūpuna	ancestors
Urupatu	utterly destroy
Waiata	a song
Wairua	spirit
Wairuatanga	spirituality
Waka	canoe
Waka ama	canoe sport
Wānanga	place of learning
Whakamārama	explanation
Whakapapa	a genealogy or family tree
Whānau	family, extended family
Whanaungatanga	kinship, relationship
Whare wānanga	house for instruction, also tribal university
Whenua	land, ground, country

Bibliography

Ahluwalia, P. 2001. *Politics and Post-colonial Theory: African Inflections.* London: Routledge.

Agreement between New Zealand and Singapore on a Closer Economic Partnership. www.mfat.govt.nz/foreign/regions/sea/singcep5.html (accessed 9 August 2002).

Ajwani, S., Blakely, T., Robson, B., Atkinson, J. and Kiro, C. 2003a. 'Unlocking the Numerator-denominator Bias III: Adjustment Ratios for 1981–1999 Mortality Data. The New Zealand Census – Mortality Study.' *New Zealand Medical Journal.* Vol. 116, no. 1175. http://www.nzma.org.nz/journal/116-1175/456/ (accessed 18 September 2006).

Ajwani, S., Blakely, T., Robson, B., Tobias, M. and Bonne, M. 2003b. *Decades of Disparity: Ethnic Mortality Trends in New Zealand 1980–1999.* Wellington: Ministry of Health and University of Otago.

Allen, C. 2002. *Blood Narrative: Indigenous Identity in American Indian and Maori Literary and Activist Texts.* Durham: Duke University Press.

American Indian Law Alliance. 2005. 'Indigenous Peoples Movement Alarmed by New Zealand's Policy.' Press Release, 9 December. http://www.scoop. co.nz/stories/WO0512/S00209.htm (accessed 21 December 2005).

Anaya, J. 2004. *Indigenous Peoples in International Law.* 2nd edn. New York: Oxford University Press.

Aotearoa Educators. 2000a. 'Potential Threat to Singaporean Investment by Maori.' Press Release, 4 August.

Aotearoa Educators. 2000b. 'Prague Style Protests to Hit Aotearoa if Singapore Deal Continues.' Press Release, 26 September.

Apirana Mahuika et al v New Zealand. Communication No 547/1993. 27 October 2000. Report of the Human Rights Committee. Vol II A/56/40.

Appadurai, A. 2000. 'Grassroots Globalization and Research Imagination.' *Public Culture.* Vol. 12, No. 1.

Bargh, M. 2002. 'Re-colonisation and Indigenous Resistance: Neoliberalism in the Pacific.' Unpublished PhD thesis, Australian National University.

Barnet, R. and Cavanagh, J. 1996. 'Electronic Money and the Casino Economy', in J. Mander and E. Goldsmith (eds) *The Case Against the Global Economy and For a Turn Toward the Local.* San Francisco: Sierra Club Books.

Barry, A., Osborne T. and Rose N. (eds) 1996. *Foucault and Political Reason.* Chicago: University of Chicago Press.

Baxter, H. 1987. *The Other Side of Dawn.* Wellington: Spiral.

Bello, W. 2005. *Deglobalization: Ideas for a New World Economy.* London: Zed Books.

Berry, R. 2005. 'Maori Denied Rights, UN Man Told.' *New Zealand Herald,* 21 November.

Bourdieu, P. 1998. 'Utopia of Endless Exploitation.' *Le Monde Diplomatique.* www.monde-diplomatique.fr/en/1998/12/08bourdieu.html (accessed 15 October 2002).

Brownlie, I. 2003. *Principles of Public International Law.* 6th edn. Oxford: Oxford University Press.

Burchell, G., Gordon, C. and Miller, P. (eds) 1991. *The Foucault Effect: Studies in Governmentality.* London: Harvester Wheatsheaf.

Campaign Against Foreign Control of Aotearoa/New Zealand. http://canterbury.cyberplace.org.nz/community/CAFCA/ (accessed 10 August 2002).

Cassese, A. 2004. *International Law.* 2nd edn. Oxford: Oxford University Press.

Charters, C. 2005. 'Developments in International Law on Indigenous Peoples' Rights and their Domestic Implications.' *NZULR.* Vol. 21, No. 4.

Chen, M. 2006. 'Maori Push Over Treaty May End in Court.' *New Zealand Herald,* 27 March.

Chossudovsky, M. 1997. *The Globalisation of Poverty.* Manilla: Institute of Political Economy.

Choudry, A. 1996. 'APEC, Free Trade, and "Economic Sovereignty".' November. http://aotearoa.wellington.net.nz/int/chondry1.html (accessed 9 January 2007).

Choudry, A. 2001. 'Bringing it all Back Home: Anti-Globalisation Activism Cannot Ignore Colonial Realities.' Z net commentary, *Z Magazine,* 3 August. http://www.zmag.org/Sustainers/content/2001-08/03choudry.htm (accessed 8 October 2002).

Churchill, W. 1994. *Indians are Us? Culture and Genocide in Native North America.* Monroe: Common Courage Press.

Convention on Biodiversity. 1992. http://www.biodiv.org/default.shtml (accessed 9 January 2007).

Crown Forest Rental Trust. 2005. Hui held at Waitangi, July 2005. http://www.cfrt.org.nz/storehouse/publications/july05newsletter.asp (accessed 18 September 2006).

Cunningham, C., Durie, M., Fergusson, D., Fitzgerald, E., Hong, B., Horwood, J., Jensen, J., Rochford, M. and Stevenson, B. 2002. *Nga Ahuatanga Noho o te Hunga Pakeke Maori: Living Standards of Older Maori 2002*. Wellington: Ministry of Social Development.

Dalziel, P. 1993. *Taxing the Poor: Key Economic Assumptions behind the April 1991 Benefit Cuts: What Are the Alternatives?* Canterbury: Department of Economics, Lincoln University.

Dansey, H. 1974. *Te Raukura: The Feathers of the Albatross*. Auckland: Longman Paul.

de Certeau, M. 1984. *The Practice of Everyday Life*. Berkeley: University of California Press.

Durie, M. 1994. *Whaiora: Maori Health Development*. Auckland: Oxford University Press.

Durie, M. 2001. A Framework for Considering Maori Educational Advancement. Opening Address at the Hui Taumata Matauranga, Turangi Aotearoa New Zealand, 24 February.

Durie, M. 2005. 'Tino Rangatiratanga', in M. Belgrave, M. Kawharu and D. Williams (eds) *Waitangi Revisited*. Melbourne: Oxford University Press.

Durie, M., Allan, G., Cunningham, C., Edwards, W., Gillies, A., Kingi, T. R., Ratima, M. and Waldon, J. 1996. *Oranga Kaumatua – A report prepared for the Ministry of Health and Te Puni Kokiri*. TPH96/3. Palmerston North: Te Pumanawa Hauora, Massey University.

Engler, A. 1995. *Apostles of Greed: Capitalism and the Myth of the Individual in the Market*. London: Pluto Press.

Fanon, F. 1990. *The Wretched of the Earth*. London: Penguin.

Federation of Maori Authorities (FOMA) website. http://www.foma.co.nz/about_foma/index.htm (accessed 18 September 2006).

Foucault, M. 1983. 'The Subject and Power', in H. L. Dreyfus and P. Rabinow, *Michel Foucault: Beyond Structuralism and Hermeneutics*. 2nd edn. Chicago: University of Chicago Press.

Foucault, M. 1991. 'Truth and Power', in P. Rabinow (ed.) *The Foucault Reader*. London: Penguin.

Foucault, M. 1994. 'The Birth of Biopolitics', in P. Rabinow (ed.) *Michel Foucault Ethics, Subjectivity and Truth, Vol. 1*. London: Penguin.

Foucault, M. 1997. 'The Ethics of the Concern of the Self as a Practice of Freedom', in P. Rabinow (ed.) *Ethics, Subjectivity and Truth*. London: Penguin.

Friedman, M. 1962. *Capitalism and Freedom*. Chicago: The University of Chicago Press.

Gallagher, J. and Robinson, R. 1953. 'The Imperialism of Free Trade.' *The Economic History Review*. Vol. 6, No. 1.

Gibson-Graham, J. K. 1996. *The End of Capitalism As We Knew It. A Feminist Critique of Political Economy*. Oxford: Blackwell Publishers.

Grace, P. 2000. 'We Write What We Know.' *Te Pua*. No. 1.

Grace, P. 2001. *Dogside Story*. Auckland: Penguin.

Grace, P. 2004. *Tu*. Auckland: Penguin.

Gramsci, A. 1997. 'The Intellectuals', in *Selections from the Prison Notebooks*, New York: International Publishers.

Harris, A. 2004. *Hikoi: Forty Years of Maori Protest*. Wellington: Huia Publishers.

Hayek, F. A. 1988. *The Fatal Conceit: The Errors of Socialism*. London: Routledge.

Hereniko, V. 1993. 'An Interview with Albert Wendt.' *Manoa*. Vol. 5, No. 1.

Hindess, B. 1996a. *Discourses of Power: From Hobbes to Foucault*. Oxford: Blackwell Publishers.

Hindess, B. 1996b. 'Liberalism, Socialism and Democracy: Variations on a Governmental Theme', in A. Barry, T. Osborne and N. Rose (eds) *Foucault and Political Reason*. Chicago: University of Chicago Press.

Hindess, B. 1997. 'A Society Governed by Contract?' in G. Davis, B. Sullivan and A.Yeatman (eds) *The New Contractualism*. Brisbane: Centre for Australia Public Sector Management.

Hindess, B. 2001a. 'Not a Home in the Empire.' *Social Identities*. Vol. 7, No. 3.

Hindess, B. 2001b. 'The Liberal Government of Unfreedom.' *Alternatives*. No. 26.

Hindess, B. 2002. 'Neo-liberal Citizenship.' *Citizenship Studies*. Vol. 6, No. 2.

Hindess, B. 2006. 'Terrortory.' Unpublished paper.

Horsfield, A. and Evans, M. 1988. *Maori Women in the Economy: A Preliminary Review of the Economic Position of Maori Women in New Zealand*. Wellington: Te Ohu Whakatupu, Te Minitatanga mo nga Wahine.

Howden-Chapman, P. and Wilson, N. 2000a. 'Housing and Health', in P. Howden-Chapman and M. Tobias (eds) *Social Inequalities in Health: New Zealand 1999*. Wellington: Ministry of Health.

Howden-Chapman, P. and Tobias, M (eds) 2000b. *Social Inequalities in Health: New Zealand 1999*. Wellington: Ministry of Health.

Hughes, A. V. 1998. *A Different Kind of Voyage: Development and Dependence in the Pacific Islands*. Manila: Office of Pacific Operations, Asian Development Bank.

Huia Publishers. 1995a. 'He Kupu Whakataki.' *Ngā Pakiwaitara a Huia 1995*. Wellington: Huia.

Huia Publishers. 1995b. *Huia Short Stories 1995*. Wellington: Huia.

Hui Taumata website. http://www.huitaumata.maori.nz/ (accessed 10 April 2006).

Human Rights Commission Resolution 1982/19. 10 March 1982. Economic and Social Council Resolution 1982/34. 7 May 1982. UN ESCOR 1982 Supp no 1 at 26, UN Doc E/1982/82.

Human Rights Commission. 2003. *Draft Discussion Document of the Human Rights Commission: Human Rights and the Treaty of Waitangi/Te Mana i te Waitangi*. Wellington: New Zealand Human Rights Commission.

Hyman, P. 2004. 'Critique of the Proposed Chile/New Zealand Closer Economic Partnership P3 with Singapore.' Wellington: Action Research and Education Network of Aotearoa (ARENA). Available on the ARENA website. http://www.arena.org.nz/chilefta.pdf (accessed 2 February 2006).

Ihimaera, W. (ed.) 1993. *Te Ao Marama 2: Te Whakahuatanga o te Ao*. Auckland: Reed.

Ihimaera, W. 1996. 'Kaupapa', in W. Ihimaera (ed.) *Te Ao Marama 5: Te Torino*. Auckland: Reed.

Ihimaera, W. 2000. *The Uncle's Story*. Auckland: Penguin.

Ihimaera, W. 2003. *Pounamu Pounamu*. Auckland: Reed.

Ihimaera, W. 2004. *Whanau II*. Auckland: Reed.

Ihimaera, W. and Grace, P. 1978. 'The Maori in Literature', in M. King (ed.) *Tihei Mauri Ora: Aspects of Maoritanga*. Auckland: Methuen.

International Monetary Fund. 'Statutory Purposes', and 'Articles of Agreement of the International Monetary Fund, Article I, Purposes.' http://www.imf.org (accessed 14 October 2002).

Indigenous Peoples' Centre for Documentation, Research and Information. 2004. 'Update 59–69.' July/October. DoCip website. http://www.docip.org/anglais/update_en/index.html (accessed 2 January 2005).

International Covenant on Civil and Political Rights. 1966. 999 UNTS 171. 19 December.

International Labour Organisation. 1989. International Labour Organisation Convention 169 Concerning Indigenous and Tribal Peoples in Independent Countries. 27 June.

Jackson, M. 1993. 'Land Loss and the Treaty of Waitangi', in W. Ihimaera (ed.) *Te Ao Marama: Regaining Aotearoa: Maori Writers Speak Out. Volume 2. He Whakaatanga o te Ao: The Reality*. Auckland: Reed Books.

Jackson, M. 1995. 'Comment', in G. McLay (ed.) *Treaty Settlements*. Wellington: New Zealand Institute of Advanced Legal Studies.

Jefferies, P. A. 2000. 'Human Rights, Foreign Policy and Religious Belief: An Asia/Pacific Perspective.' *BYU Law Review*. Vol. 883.

Joannemariebarker and Teaiwa, T. 1998. 'Native Information.' *Inscriptions*. Vol. 7.

Jones, C. 1999. *Maori-Pakeha Health Disparities. Can Treaty Settlements Reverse the Impacts of Racism?* Wellington: Ian Axford Fellowships Office.

Kawharu, I. H. (ed.) 1989. *Waitangi: Maori and Pakeha Perspectives of the Treaty of Waitangi*. Auckland: Oxford University Press.

Kawharu, M. (ed.) 2002. *Whenua: Managing Our Resources*. Auckland: Reed.

Kelsey, J. 1999. *Reclaiming the Future*. Auckland: Bridget Williams Books.

Kelsey, J. 2005. 'Submission to the Foreign Affairs and Trade Select Committee on the Trans-Pacific Strategic Economic Cooperation Agreement.' November. Available on the Bilaterals.Org website. http://www.bilaterals. org/article.php3?id_article=4532 (accessed 3 August 2006).

Keynes, J. M. 1964 (1936). *The General Theory of Employment, Interest and Money*. London: Macmillan.

Khor, M. 1996. 'Global Economy and the Third World', in J. Mander and E. Goldsmith (eds) *The Case Against the Global Economy and For a Turn Toward the Local*. San Francisco: Sierra Club Books.

King, J. 2003. *Economic Determinants of Health: A Report to the Public Health Advisory Committee*. Auckland: Health Outcomes International Ltd.

Kingsbury, B. 2002. 'Competing Conceptual Approaches to Indigenous Group Issues in New Zealand Law.' *University of Toronto Law Journal*. Vol. 52.

Knapman, B. and Saldanha, C. D. 1999. *Reforms in the Pacific*. Manila: Asian Development Bank.

Kohere, R. T. 1951. *The Autobiography of a Maori*. Wellington: Reed.

Köhler, H. 2001. Promoting Stability and Prosperity in a Globalised World. Paper presented at the Council of the Americas, Washington DC, 7 May 2001. http://www.imf.org/external/np/speeches/2001/050701.htm (accessed 5 December 2006)

Korten, D. C. 1995. *When Corporations Rule the World*. Connecticut: Kumarian Press.

Korten, D. C. 2000. *The Post-Corporate World: Life After Capitalism*. Sydney: Pluto Press.

Kouka, H. 1999. *Ta Matou Mangai; Three Plays of the 1990s*. Wellington: Victoria University Press.

Kunitz, S. 1994. *Disease and Social Diversity: The European Impact on the Health of Non-Europeans*. New York: Oxford University Press.

LaDuke, W. 1999. *All our Relations: Native Struggles for Land and Life*. Cambridge: South End Press.

Landry, D. and Maclean, G (eds) 1996. *The Spivak Reader: Selected works of Gayatri Chakravorty Spivak*. New York and London: Routledge.

Lappé, F. M. and Collins, J. 1998. *World Hunger: 12 Myths*. London: Earthscan.

Larmour, P. 1997. 'Corruption and Governance in the South Pacific.' *Pacific Studies*. Vol. 20, No. 3.

Larmour, P. and Wolanin, N. (eds) 2001. *Corruption and Anti-Corruption*, Canberra: Asia Pacific Press.

Lashley, M. E. 2000. 'Implementing Treaty Settlements via Indigenous Institutions: Social Justice and Detribalization in New Zealand.' *The Contemporary Pacific*. Vol. 12, No. 1.

Lewin, K. 1951. *Field Theory in Social Service: Selected Theoretical Papers*. New York: Harper Brothers.

Maaka, R. 1994. 'The New Tribe: Conflicts and Continuities in the Social Organisation of Urban Maori.' *The Contemporary Pacific*. Vol. 6, No. 2.

Mander, J. and Goldsmith, E. (eds) 1996. *The Case Against the Global Economy and For a Turn Toward the Local*. San Francisco: Sierra Club Books.

Marjoram, T. (ed.) 1994. *Island Technology: Technology for Development in the South Pacific*. London: Intermediate Technology Publications.

McCarthy, M. 1997. 'Raising a Maori Child Under a New Right State', in P. Te Whaiti, M. McCarthy and A. Durie (eds) *Mai i Rangiatea: Maori Wellbeing and Development*. Auckland: Auckland University Press.

McMaster, J. 1993. 'Strategies to Stimulate Private Sector Development in the Pacific Island Economies', in R. Cole and S. Tambunlertchai (eds) *The Future of Asia-Pacific Economies: Pacific Islands at the Crossroads?* Canberra: National Centre for Development Studies, Australian National University.

McRae, J. 1991. 'Selected Stories: Review.' *Landfall*. Issue 179.

Mehta, U. S. 1999. *Liberalism and Empire*. Chicago: University of Chicago Press.

Melbourne, H. 1995. *Maori Sovereignty: The Maori Perspective*. Auckland: Hodder Moa Beckett.

Mill, J. S. 1975. *Three Essays: On Liberty, Representative Government, The Subjection of Women*. Oxford: Oxford University Press.

Minh-ha, Trinh, T. 1989. *Woman, Native, Other*. Bloomington: Indiana University Press.

Ministry of Foreign Affairs and Trade. 'An Initial Analysis on the Trade and Economic Benefits of Negotiating a "Pacific Three" Closer Economic Partnership Agreement Involving Chile.' www.mfat.govt.nz/foreign/tnd/ceps/cepchilenzsing/chilenzsingcep1.html (accessed 31 May 2005).

Ministry of Foreign Affairs and Trade. 1999. 'New Zealand Negotiating Brief on the Draft Declaration on the Rights of Indigenous Peoples.' Wellington: New Zealand Government.

Ministry of Foreign Affairs and Trade. 2005. 'National Interest Analysis: Trans-Pacific Strategic Economic Cooperation Agreement.' Wellington: Ministry of Foreign Affairs and Trade.

Ministry of Health. 2002a. *Cancer in New Zealand: Trends and Projections*. Wellington: Ministry of Health.

Ministry of Health. 2002b. *He Korowai Oranga: Maori Health Strategy*. Wellington: Ministry of Health.

Mita, M. 1992. 'The Soul and the Image', in J. Dennis and J. Bieringa (eds) *Film in Aotearoa New Zealand*. Wellington: Victoria University Press.

Mita, M. 1993. 'Indigenous Literature in a Colonial Society', in W. Ihimaera (ed.) *Te Ao Marama 2: He Whakaatanga o te Ao*. Auckland: Reed.

Mudrooroo. 1995. *Us Mob: History, Culture, Struggle: An introduction to Indigenous Australia*. Sydney: Angus & Robertson.

Mutu, M. 2004a. Keynote Address at Matauranga Tuku Iho Tikanga Rangahau. Traditional Knowledge and Research Ethics Conference 2004. Te Papa, Wellington, 10–12 June 2004. Auckland: Nga Pae o te Maramatanga.

Mutu, M. 2004b. Submission on the Foreshore and Seabed Bill. Fisheries and Other Sea Related Legislation Select Committee, 2004. http://www.clerk. parliament.govt.nz/content/Select_Committee_Submissions/Fisheries_ and_other_Sea_related_Legislation_Committee/Foreshore_and_ Seabed_Bill/M_to_N/Mutu%20M%200291.pdf (accessed 28 April 2006).

Nandy, A. 1983. *The Intimate Enemy: Loss and Recovery of Self Under Colonialism*. Oxford: Oxford University Press.

National Council of Teachers of English Convention. 1994. 'Patricia Grace Describes Her Writing and Her Maori Ancestry.' *College English* (Pittsburgh).

National Health Committee. 1998. *The Social, Cultural and Economic Determinants of Health in New Zealand: Action to Improve Health*. Wellington: National Advisory Committee on Health and Disability.

National Health Committee. 2002. *National Advisory Committee on Health and Disability 11th Annual Report to the Minister of Health*. Wellington: National Health Committee.

New Zealand Health Information Service. 2004. *Suicide Facts. Provisional 2001 Statistics. All Ages*. Wellington: New Zealand Health Information Service.

New Zealand Maori Council v Attorney-General [1987] 1 NZLR.

Office of the High Commissioner for Human Rights. 1995. 'Report of the Working Group Established in Accordance with the Commission on Human Rights Resolution 1995/32 of 3 March 1995 on its Tenth Session.' http://daccessdds.un.org/doc/UNDOC/GEN/G05/157/58/PDF/G0515758.pdf?OpenElement (accessed 14 January 2006).

Office of Treaty Settlements. 2002. *Healing a Past, Building a Future.* Wellington: Office of Treaty Settlements, Ministry of Justice.

Orange, C. 1987. *The Treaty of Waitangi.* Wellington: Allen & Unwin Port Nicholson Press with assistance from the Historical Publications Branch, Department of Internal Affairs.

Orbell, M. 1970. *Contemporary Maori Writing.* Wellington: Reed.

Ormerod, P. 1995. *The Death of Economics.* London: Faber and Faber.

Otter, M. 1994. 'Privatisation: An Agenda for the South Pacific.' *Pacific Economic Bulletin* (Canberra: Asia Pacific Press). Vol. 9, No. 1.

Park, G. 1995. *Nga Uruora: Ecology and History in a New Zealand Landscape.* Wellington: Victoria University Press.

Patuawa-Nathan, E. 1979. *Opening Doors: A Collection of Poems.* Suva: Mana Publications.

Peace Movement Aotearoa 2006. 'Act Now for Indigenous Peoples' Rights.' Wellington: Peace Movement Aotearoa.

Peoples' Global Action Against 'Free' Trade and the World Trade Organisation. http://www.agp.org (accessed 6 October 2002).

Pomare, E., Keefe-Ormsby, V., Ormsby, C., Pearce, N., Reid, P., Robson, B. and Watene-Haydon, N. 1995. *Hauora: Maori Standards of Health. A Study of the Years 1970–1991.* Wellington: Te Ropu Rangahau Hauora a Eru Pomare.

Pool, I. 1991. *Te Iwi Maori: A New Zealand Population Past, Present and Projected.* Auckland: Auckland University Press.

Potiki, R. 1991. 'Introduction', in S. Garrett (ed.) *He Reo Hou; 5 Plays by Maori Playwrights.* Wellington: Playmarket.

Potiki, R. 1993. 'The Journey from Anxiety to Confidence', in W. Ihimaera (ed.) *Te Ao Marama 2: He Whakaatanga o te Ao.* Auckland: Reed.

Press (Christchurch). 2004. 'Ngai Tahu Wins Pacific Support.' 14 May.

Pritchard, S. 1998. 'Native Title from the Perspective of International Standards.' *Australian Yearbook of International Law.* Vol. 18, No. 127.

Radcliffe, S., Laurie, N. and Andoline, R. 2002. 'Indigenous Peoples and Political Transnationalism: Globalisation from Below Meets Globalisation from Above.' http://www.transcomm.ox.ac.uk/working%20papers/WPTC-02-05%20Radcliffe.pdf (accessed 20 December 2005).

Reid, P. and Pouwhare, R. 1991. *Te Taonga-mai-Tawhiti: The gift from a distant place*. Auckland: Niho Taniwha.

Reid, P., Robson, B. and Jones, C. P. 2000. 'Disparities in Health: Common Myths and Uncommon Truths.' *Pacific Health Dialog*. Vol. 7.

Ricardo, D. 1987 (1817). *The Principles of Political Economy and Taxation*. London: Everyman's Library.

Rika-Heke, P. 1996. 'Margin or Center? Let Me Tell You! In the Land of My Ancestors I Am the Center: Indigenous Writing in Aotearoa', in R. Mohanram and G. Rajan (eds) *English Postcoloniality: Literatures from Around the World*. Westport, CT: Greenwood.

Riki, J. 1999. 'Te Wa Kainga: "Home"', in P. Abood, B. Gamba and M. Kotevski (eds) *Waiting in Space: An Anthology of Australian Writing*. Annandale NSW: Pluto Press.

Rio Declaration on Environment and Development, 1999. UN Conference on Environment and Development, Rio de Janeiro, 13 June. UN Doc A/ CONF.151/26.vol 1. Annex 1.

Robinson, T. 2003. 'The Cost to the New Zealand Government of Providing "Free" Primary Medical Care: An Estimate Based upon the Rand Health Insurance Experiment.' *New Zealand Medical Journal*. Vol. 116.

Robson, B. 2002. *Mana Whakamaarama. Equal Explanatory Power*. Wellington: Te Ropu Rangahau Hauora a Eru Pomare.

Robson, B. 2004. 'The Economic Determinants of Maori Health and Disparities.' A review for Te Ropu Tohutohu i te Hauora Tumatanui, Public Health Advisory Committee. Wellington: Te Ropu Rangahau Hauora a Eru Pomare.

Rojas, C. 2001. Governing Through the Social: The Role of International Financial Institutions in the Third World. A paper presented at the International Studies Association meeting, Chicago, 21 February.

Rojas, C. 2002. *Civilization and Violence: Regimes of Representation in Nineteenth-Century Colombia*. Minneapolis: University of Minnesota.

Rosenberg, B. 1999. Foreign Investment and APEC. A paper presented to the forum Alternatives to the APEC Agenda, Christchurch, 24 April.

Royal Commission on Genetic Modification. 2001. *Report of the Royal Commission on Genetic Modification,* Wellington: Royal Commission on Genetic Modification.

Said, E. W. 1993. *Culture and Imperialism*. New York: Vintage.

Said, E. W. 1994. *Representations of the Intellectual: The 1993 Reith Lectures*. London: Vintage.

Samuels, W. J. (ed.) 1990. *Economics as Discourse: An Analysis of the Language of Economics*. Boston: Kluwer Academic Publishers.

Scott, J. C. 1985. *Weapons of the Weak*. New Haven: Yale University Press.

Shapiro, M. J. 1993. *Reading 'Adam Smith': Desire, History and Value*. London: Sage Publications.

Shaw, M. N. 2003. *International Law*. 5th edn. Cambridge: Cambridge University Press.

Shiva, V. and Holla-Bhar, R. 1996. 'Piracy by Patent: The Case of the Neem Tree', in J. Mander and E. Goldsmith (eds) *The Case Against the Global Economy and For a Turn Toward the Local*. San Francisco: Sierra Club Books.

Sillitoe, P. 1997. 'Pacific Values and the Economics of Land Use: A Response to Bayliss-Smith', in B. Burt and C. Clerk (eds) *Environment and Development in the Pacific Islands*. Canberra: National Centre for Development Studies, Australian National University.

Smith, A. 1872 (1776). *An Inquiry Into The Nature And Causes of The Wealth of Nations*. Edinburgh: Adam and Charles Black.

Smith, L. 1999. *Decolonizing Methodologies, Research and Indigenous Peoples*. Dunedin: University of Otago Press.

Solomos, J. and Back, L. 1996. *Racism and Society*. Houndmills: Macmillan Press.

Spivak, G. 1999. *A Critique of Postcolonial Reason: Toward a History of the Vanishing Present*. Cambridge and London: Harvard University Press.

Stead, C. K. 1966. *New Zealand Short Stories: Second Series*. London, Wellington: Oxford University Press.

Stiglitz, J. 1999. 'Trade and the Developing World: A New Agenda.' *Current History*, November.

Sturm, J. C. 1983. *House of the Talking Cat: Stories*. Wellington: Spiral.

Sullivan, R. 2005. *Voice Carried My Family*. Auckland: Auckland University Press.

Teaiwa, T. 1999. 'Scholarship from a Lazy Native.' *Moana*. Vol. 4, Spring.

Te Puni Kokiri. 1997a. *ACC's Service Delivery: Maori claimant and provider Perspectives. Key Findings*. Wellington: Te Puni Kokiri.

Te Puni Kokiri. 1997b. *Kia Mohio*. No. 2, July. Wellington.

Te Puni Kokiri. 2000a. *Maori in the New Zealand Economy*. 2nd edn. Wellington: Te Puni Kokiri.

Te Puni Kokiri. 2000b. *Progress Towards Closing Social and Economic Gaps between Maori and non-Maori: A Report to the Minister of Maori Affairs May 2000*. Wellington: Te Puni Kokiri.

Te Puni Kokiri. 2001a. *He Tirohanga o Kawa ti te Tiriti o Waitangi: A Guide to the Principles of the Treaty of Waitangi as expressed by the Court and the Waitangi Tribunal*. Wellington: Te Puni Kokiri.

Te Puni Kokiri. 2001b. *The Quality of Teacher Training for Teaching Maori Students.* Wellington: Te Puni Kokiri.

Te Ropu Rangahau Hauora a Eru Pomare. 2000. 'Counting for Nothing: Understanding the Issues in Monitoring Disparities.' *Social Policy Journal of New Zealand.* Vol. 14.

Te Runanga o Whare Kauri Rekoku Inc v Attorney General. 12 October 1992. HC WN CP 682/92 Heron J.

Tipene-Leach, D., Abel, S., Finau, S., Park, J. and Lenna, M. 2000. 'Maori Infant Care Practices: Implications for Health Messages, Infant Care Services and SIDS Prevention in Maori Communities.' *Pacific Health Dialog.* Vol. 7.

Trans-Pacific Strategic Economic Partnership Agreement. http://www.mfat. govt.nz/tradeagreements/transpacepa/transpacsepindex.html (accessed 28 April 2006).

Trask, H. K. 1993. *From a Native Daughter: Colonialism and Sovereignty in Hawai'i.* Maine: Common Courage Press.

Tukuitonga, C. and Bindman, A. 2002. Ethnic and Gender Differences in the Use of Coronary Artery Revascularisation Procedures in New Zealand. *New Zealand Medical Journal.* Vol. 115.

Tuwhare, H. 1964. *No Ordinary Sun.* Auckland: Blackwood and Janet Paul.

United Nations. 2000. *World Economic and Social Survey.* New York: Department of Economic and Social Information and Policy Analysis, United Nations.

United Nations Committee on the Elimination of All Forms of Racial Discrimination. 1997. 'General Recommendation XXIII: Indigenous Peoples.' 18 August. A/52/18.

United Nations Committee on the Elimination of All Forms of Racial Discrimination. 1999. 'Decision 2.54. on Australia.' 18 March. A/54/18.

United Nations Committee on the Elimination of All Forms of Racial Discrimination. 2005. 'Decision 1.66.: New Zealand Foreshore and Seabed Act 2004.' 11 March. CERD/C/66/NZL/Dec.1.

United Nations Conference on Trade and Development. 2001. *FDI in Developing Countries at a Glance.* Geneva: United Nations.

United Nations Declaration on the Rights of Indigenous Peoples. http://www. ohchr.org/english/issues/indigenous/docs/declaration.doc (accessed 9 January 2007).

United Nations Development Programme. 1999. *Human Development Report: Globalization With a Human Face.* Oxford: Oxford University Press.

United Nations High Commission for Human Rights. 2003. 'Norms on the Responsibilities of Transnational Corporations and Other Business Enterprises with Regard to Human Rights.' http://www. unhchr.ch/huridocda/huridoca.nsf/.Symbol./E.CN.4.Sub.2.2003.12. Rev.2.En?Opendocument (accessed 14 January 2006).

United Nations Special Rapporteur on the Situation of Human Rights and Fundamental Freedoms of Indigenous Peoples. 2006. 'Indigenous Issues.' E/CN.4/2006/78/1dd.3. Economic and Social Council. VI, 84.

Urrehman, S. 2001. 'On the Impossibility of Constructing a Postcolonial Praxis', in G. Ratcliffe and G. Turcotte (eds) *Compromising Post/colonialisms*. Sydney: Dangaroo Press.

Waitangi Tribunal. http://www.waitangi-tribunal.govt.nz/ (accessed 21 December 2005).

Waligorski, C. 1990. *The Political Theory of Conservative Economists*. Kansas: University Press of Kansas.

Walker, R. 1990. *Ka Whawhai Tonu Matou. Struggle Without End*. Auckland: Penguin Books.

Walker, R. 1996. *Nga Pepa a Ranginui, The Walker Papers*. Auckland: Penguin Books.

Warf, B. 2000. 'Telecommunications and Economic Space', in E. Sheppard and T. J. Barnes (eds) *A Companion to Economic Geography*. Oxford: Blackwell.

Wellington International Airport Ltd v Air New Zealand [1993] 1 NZLR 671.

Westbrooke, I., Baxter, J. and Hogan, J. 2000. 'Are Maori Under-served for Cardiac Interventions?' *New Zealand Medical Journal*. Vol. 114.

Whaitiri, R. and Sullivan, R. 1997. 'The Forest of Tane: Maori Literature Today.' *Manoa*. Vol. 9, No. 1.

Williams, D. 1999. 'Constructing the Economic Space: The World Bank and the Making of Homo Oeconomicus.' *Millennium: Journal of International Studies*. Vol. 28, No. 1.

Williams, D. 2001. *Matauranga Maori and Taonga: The Nature and Extent of Treaty Rights Held by Iwi and Hapu in Indigenous Flora and Fauna, Cultural Heritage and Objects, Valued Traditional Knowledge*. Wellington: Waitangi Tribunal.

Williams, D. R. 1996. 'Race/Ethnicity and Socioeconomic Status: Measurement and Methodological Issues.' *International Journal of Health Services*. Vol. 26.

Williams, D. R. 1997. 'Race and Health: Basic Questions, Emerging Directions.' *Annals of Epidemiology*. Vol. 7.

Williams, D. R. 2002. 'Racial/Ethnic Variations in Women's Health: The Social Embeddedness of Health.' *American Journal of Public Health*. Vol. 92.

Williams, H. W. 1985. *A Dictionary of the Maori Language*. Wellington: Government Printer.

Williams, L. and O'Brien, M. 2003. *The Dynamics of Debt for Low Income Families*. Wellington: New Zealand Council of Christian Social Services.

Womack, C. 1999. *Red on Red: Native American Literary Separatism*. Minneapolis: Minnesota University Press.

World Bank. 1998. *Pacific Islands Regional Economic Report.* Manila: East Asia and Pacific Division.

World Bank. 2002. *Pacific Islands Regional Economic Report: Embarking on a Global Voyage: Trade Liberalization and Complementary Reforms in the Pacific.* Manila: Poverty Reduction and Economic Management Unit, East Asia and Pacific Region.

World Trade Organisation. 'Understanding the WTO: Settling Disputes.' http://www.wto.org/english/thewto_e/whatis_e/tif_e/disp1_e.htm (accessed 28 April 2006).

Young, R. J. C. 2001. *Postcolonialism.* Oxford: Blackwell.

Index